A MOUNTAIN FARMHOUSE.

IN LAKELAND DELLS
AND FELLS

BY

W. T. PALMER

AUTHOR OF 'LAKE-COUNTRY RAMBLES,' ETC

LONDON
CHATTO & WINDUS
1903

CONTENTS

v

CONTENTS

SHEPHERD LIFE AMONG THE FELLS

SHEPHERD LIFE AMONG THE FELLS

I. A Link with the Past

A VOLUNTARY exile from the land of the fells is an old-time shepherd. Instead of among heathery wastes or rocky scaurs, he lives between dismal gray grass-slopes where the Pennine divides Lancashire and Yorkshire. Probably the heart beating within that stout framework which defied the mountain storms of fifty years ago oft turns from the new pursuits to the old. I met him on a cobbled road—what an abomination these inhospitable stones must be to one whose foot for long fell soft and silent on the grass of the uplands!—a weathered, well-made man, with hair and whiskers turning tardily from brown to gray.

Shortly he detected that I knew and loved his own native land of the fells, and then, after rapidly reviewing scenes from many a lovely lake and valley there, our talk lighted upon some phase of shepherdry; and then his eye kindled, and I knew him for what he truly was—a shepherd.

3   A 2

'You know that dale, eh? I well remember the time when all the high fells you can see from it were open and common to its farmers. Now they are cut up according to the size of the holdings.

'Before that happened the shepherd's work was much more difficult. Sheep-smits were a real thing then ; you *had* to know the mark of every farm for miles round, for, unhindered by fences, strays were always coming and going. Lambing-time was often late in May, and a hard time it was. The shepherd had to remain night and day with his flock, oft in a far-off mountain basin, where for a fortnight on end he might never meet a single person. If the weather came stormy, the labour and anxiety was trebled ; the ewes and lambs had to be seen to at all cost. One time I was four days and five nights without rest, for first a great blizzard and then a wild rain-storm raged. In my flock alone forty ewes died in those four days ; the total loss of lambs was impossible to reckon, for the whole lambing was spoiled. And I was in a sheltered position, too. At such times, and when we worked the highest grass at midsummer, our food had to be brought up to some pre-arranged spot—a rough hut made with turf and a few spruce branches, partially sheltering under some big rock. Often for two or three summer nights, when it was fine, we lay out on the open moor. If a spell of really wet weather set in, of course we came down nearer to the dales. During a thunder-storm we frequently were in danger. I have seen a score sheep struck with lightning—what a horrid smell is that of burning flesh and wool!

'At all times, fair weather or foul, our work was greatly lightened by our dogs. It is a pleasure for a shepherd to train them for his own use. You can't buy a first-rate sheep-dog with gold. When I began shepherding, sheep were much wilder than now, less in size, carrying but poor wool, thriving badly. Cross-breeding with the Scotch sheep has imparted a good deal of vigour to the mountain flocks, and the blood of Southern breeds shows in increased size and choicer wool. Often when wandering along the fellsides we shepherds used to sight one another, but, seeing that each had a flock of about four thousand, it wasn't likely that we could feed our sheep together. If we did come close, our flocks quickly got mixed, and there was half a day's work sorting them again. In those days, too, as wool fetched a better price on the market by about double what it does now, shepherding was the best-paying farm work. So there were plenty of good fellsmen to be got—men that could clip [shear] and wash and doctor with the best there is to-day.

'How did we manage to divide the fell up without fences? As I have said, every farm had the right to send a number of sheep to graze on the fell in those days, as they have a claim on so many acres of pasture now. The owners of adjoining smaller farms combined to employ a shepherd among them. Of course, the bigger halls kept shepherds of their own. For farms on the right-side of the valley the shepherd claimed the land from their outermost wall up to the top of the watershed for width, and for length as far as the lowland extended. A shepherd might thus drive over a moor four miles long and six miles wide, with perhaps occasional excursions some eight or more miles.

'A shepherd's first job in the spring was to collect the sheep, and to get to know their marks. Then he drove the mass to where there was enough grass for pasturing. When you were walking among the fells'—addressing me more pointedly—'you would likely notice a great number of sheepfolds. These formerly marked the end of the "heafs," or pasturages. The shepherd's work was to drive his flock daily from one set of folds to the other. But, seeing that grass is sparse on these uplands—many an acre is

occupied with cliffs and beds of rock and scree—
the shepherd had constantly to vary the level of
his route.

'Soon after the flock were on the fell-grass
lambing commenced, when the more weakly of
his command needed close attention. The sheep
didn't make things any easier by wandering to
as remote positions as possible. Lambing-time
lasted four weeks as a rule, and after that the
summer grass had fully come. As the days began
to be hot, we used to let our sheep wander into
the deep dark ghylls and the narrow shadows of
the boulders while we took a nap. Sometimes,
instead of sleeping, we passed the time in trying
to avenge ourselves of our natural foes. The
raven and the fox particularly had levied toll of
the weakest of our flocks at lambing-time, and
now we had a chance.

'I have heard people say that the raven does
no harm to the flock, but simply eats up any dead
bodies that may be lying on the fells. I have
seen, and at that time knew many men who had
seen the same thing, ravens descend from the
great crags and attack newborn lambs. I say this
while believing that hawks, magpies, and carrion
crows do not do a fraction of harm to living
sheep or lambs. But to talk about any or all of
them clearing dead bodies away—it's sheer non-

sense. In three days the mountain beetles, tiny though they be, will clear every particle of flesh from a dead sheep, leaving merely a skeleton of bones and a few patches of wool. The raven is very plucky in defence of its nest, and more than once I have heard of men being attacked by them when after their nests. It's exciting work clambering about the crags on the end of a thin rope. You will maybe have seen near fox tracks and earths short walls, and perhaps even loopholed huts built of boulders. So rough are these that few save dalesfolk notice them. They are shelters for shooting from. At dawn and nightfall shepherds lie in wait in these places, and fire upon the foxes as they pass. Few of the shots are successful, owing to the poor light prevailing. The other ways of killing foxes include poison, traps, and digging them out of borrans. Many a score of fox-cubs are taken by the shepherds ; they are worth ten shillings apiece to masters of foxhounds in the low country. I have downed many a fox by finding its benk (or place where it lies out in summer), and then getting the sheepdogs to chase it into the open past me.

'The next job in our summer, of course, was washing and shearing, but it wasn't often that I had much to do with either of these. A good many sheep were drafted off about this time and sold. Big flocks were sent into Scotland, and I generally got some droving. It was in the days before railways came into this part of the world. Sheep were then sent between buyer and seller by road. I remember, perhaps, best my first journey. I was then with a farmer not so far from Shap Fells—in fact, our sheep grazed on a corner of that big common. Our master and his neighbours sold altogether five thousand sheep to go to a farm which was being newly stocked near John o' Groats—right away up in the North of Scotland. John Todd and myself were picked out to drive them, and one Friday morning we were to start. With our dogs at heel, we walked down to the lowermost farm in the dale which was sending sheep. It was a bonny morning. Skylarks, though the stars were hardly gone, were whirling up, singing as only wild birds can. The beck rattled down among the rocks and gurgled into the dubs. There had been rain in the night, and when the sun got up every grass-blade shone with wee drops. To a stranger, maybe, our dale looks wild and desolate, but to me it was home. We passed the school where I learnt my few lessons, and stopped at the next farm—old Donald Morris had it then.

 ' "Come in—come in, John !" called the old farmer, as our clog-irons rang on the paved fold.

" What, Jimmy ! is thoo gaen [going] with t'
sheep ?"

' " Ay !" I said.

' " Well, come on and have some breakfast wi'
us ; we're just sitting down."

' But I was glad John Todd said nay, for the
word " breakfast " put me by it [made me dis-
inclined].   You'll understand what it is for a
lad leaving his home-dale for the first time.
We shepherds think a lot of home, though
it means cold flagged floors, rough-beamed dark
rooms, and leaking roofs, with whitewashed
cottage walls, and maybe a straggly stick-heap
outside.

' Donald came with us, and showed us the batch
of his sheep we were to take.

' " They'll be a bit bad to manage, maybe, till
you get out of the sound of the lambs," said he.
" Here, Toss, Nell, get away by" [pass beyond the
sheep].

' In a minute the dogs had driven the tiny flock
out upon the dale-road, and there they were restlessly moving back and forward, waiting for us to
commence our long drive.

' " Noo, Jimmy," said the old man, pressing
the first crown piece of my own I had ever
possessed into my hand, " mind thoo does as
John bids thee.   I remember thy father's first

droving; it was frae here into Scotland. It's a lang while sen."

'John called "How-up!" at this juncture; the sheep started forward, and away we went. From the farmfold of Donald Morris I could see a little white cottage perched high up the brae—my home—and my heart grew sick for it. But as we began to push up the dale our flock of ewes—many of them leaving lambs on the hillsides around—began to show spirit. Every gateway they tried to rush; at a leaning or lower piece of wall one or two surely attempted to scale it. Once or twice sheep wriggled through small gaps into the fields around, and had to be hounded back to the road. All the time a babel of bleatings filled the air, our crowd replying with guttural voices to the thin wailings of the lambs.

'Every minute the row [tumult of sound] grew wilder and our sheep moved with more difficulty. Farm after farm was called at, or their shepherds joined their quota on to ours from the fields. At each place a billet of numbers and markings was given us, that we might prove our claim to any that might stray or be stolen during our journey. By about nine o'clock we reached the coach-road which leads across Shap Fell, and soon after this the flock seemed to accept the inevitable, and quietened down beautifully. Not for long, however, for immediately we came on to enclosed roads they became very lively, especially when, with a wild blare on the horn, a mail-coach passed us just above Brougham Castle. They were scared without doubt, and it took us all our time to keep up with them. Will you believe it, that by eight o clock at night we were past Carlisle? We had travelled, mainly at a run, over forty miles, and, sheep, dogs, and men alike, we were dead tired. The sheep were very hungry, too, for after leaving the open fell-road they hadn't stopped to nibble a single mouthful of grass. Next day we crossed the Border. We perhaps did not get quite so many miles done, for once our flock took a wrong road, in spite of all our dogs could do ; but, all the same, it was a hard, fast day—— What did you say?'

'Oh, I merely asked if you saw Gretna Green, where there used to be so many runaway weddings?'

'Oh ay! But there was no blacksmith's shop at the bridge end, as folk nowadays say there was. There were three or four postillions at the next public-house, laughing of how they'd driven post-haste from Penrith that morning, with two couple of gentlefolks. No doubt the gentlefolks themselves were in the house, but we didn't see them.

'After four days of hard travelling we had crossed the mountains behind Moffatt, and were getting near to Stirling. John Todd had again and again said this pace could not last, and now the sheep began to get more into command. Every day saw a mile or two less than the one before, till we got down to a steady twenty-one miles per day. The sheep were many of them quite footsore, and our dogs could hardly raise a run. I remember quite well Stirling, with its great castle pitched on top of a tall crag, and with the beck in the valley below. Now we began to rest our flock every third day, and so crossed the lowlands and approached the mountains. Folks began to stare at the English shepherds, and wherever we stopped there was a crowd to ask us questions. The country began to look different. To Perth every field was cultivated; they grew the same crops as on the lower land in Westmorland, and a fair good yield there seemed to be. So far we had been easily able to get a lodging each night, and a field to put the sheep in, but now there came to be fewer and fewer houses by the roadsides, and even inns were scarce.

'At this lapse of time I remember but few names of places; you see, the country folks pronounced them so much different to what they look in writing. One morning we left a village;

almost immediately the road began to climb into the middle of the great Grampian Mountains. Our sheep moved but lamely and slowly. At mid-day, however, we had come on to a wide moorland, the road over which was overgrown with grass from scant use. In time we came to where the stump of a guide-post marked a parting of ways, and near this stood a Highlander in kilt and tartan. He looked at our flock as it filed past, then spoke to us a bit excitedly.

'My companion knew Lowland Scotch well, and had picked up a bit of Gaelic about Perth on other journeys, but this man spoke a thick dialect which completely baffled him.

'"Are we right for Inverness?" John asked again and again, but the man's reply, though long and earnest, contained not a word we could make out. Even the name Inverness was strange to the man, and, alas! we knew not any near village. The Highlander seemed, by his signs, to wish to tell us either something about the weather or the late hour for driving, for he swung his arms again and again in the direction of the drooping sun. For some minutes we tried in vain to understand him; then John Todd said :

'"Well, Jimmy, he seemingly thinks we're on the road to somewhere, for he doesn't try to stop us. So, seeing it's getting a bit late, we must be pushing on."

'And on we went. A last backward glance showed us that the Scot had set off along the opposite route. Now hill after hill was passed; never a house in sight, only a wearying succession of gray, bare braes, with a sky growing dark. At nine o'clock we toiled up a long slope, fording a stream at its foot—just the same desolate scene. Night was fast falling, when John said:

' " Jimmy, it seems to me that that Scottie wanted to tell us it was far to the next village; but whatever it was, this is certain—we'll have to sleep out to-night. Canst thou see a hut or shelter handy for us and the dogs? The sheep won't stray far; they're overtired."

'A big boulder of granite stood some fifty yards away, and under it we lay down, wrapped in our top-coats. It was a bright night till midnight; millions of stars glittered above, and a thin horn of a moon shone. Then the weather changed. From leaving Shap Fell to here we had only had one wet day, but now it made up for lost time. The breeze blew strong and cold from the west, and a great pack of cloud flew up into the sky. It began to rain smartly; there was a sudden sharp gust of wind, and everything was blotted out in blinding mist. My! it was cold waiting up there for the dawning—colder far than a wet autumn morning on Shap Fell. I couldn't sleep, nor could the dogs, but John and our flock seemed to take the occurrence as a matter of course. The wind veered round about five o'clock, just as we were ranging up and counting the sheep—a difficult job in the half-darkness—and in ten minutes the last shred of damp cloud was torn from the ridges around and the whole moorland was ablaze with day. Perhaps the outlook at sunset had been wild and gray, but everything now was fresh and green. Cheerfulness in life seemed to be renewed everywhere ; our sheep walked less tiredlike ; our dogs frisked about merrily. At mid-day we reached a small inn. There was no occupant within, all being, probably, haymaking in some invisible field, so we foraged for ourselves : a brown loaf and some cheese made an excellent repast after a fast of over thirty-six hours. Then, leaving money on the table to appease our unwitting host, we pushed on, hoping to reach some village ere sundown, which we did. We saw our sheep safely into a field and went to bed.

'We had intended to stay two days in this place to rest our sheep, but on our very first turn-out John and I were collared and handcuffed by a couple of broad policemen. We asked again and again what we had done, but they only grunted out some words we could not understand. After ten minutes, in which a lively debate went on between the policemen, we were jerked along between them right through the village, stopping at last at a big house. A few words passed between our captors and the servant, and then the four of us were shown into a big room. Presently a big soldierly man came in; he walked with a limp, but he seemed to be a real gentleman.

'He spoke a minute with the two constables, then turned to us, and said in English:

'"Well, what have you to say?"

'"Will you first tell us what about, sir?" said John. "What's to do that we're brought here?"

'He looked a bit surprised at John's quiet way, and said:

'"You're brought here for sheep-stealing. The police tell me you have brought a lot of sheep from the moors to this village. What have you to say?"

'John laughed, and I laughed too.

'"Well if ever! Why, we've driven the sheep from Shap Fell, in Westmorland! I'll show ye my proofs." And John turned a whole pile of papers out of his pocket, which the magistrate read slowly and carefully.

'"Do you know Captain ——?" he said a moment later, naming a man well known in our district.

' " Of course I do! My father used to work for him, and so I did myself. My brother is in his regiment, sir."

' " What is your brother like, and what is his name ?"

' John of course gave these details without a bit of trouble, after which the magistrate got up and shook hands with us both, gentleman though he was.

' " Your brother is in my regiment, too," he said; " or, at least, it was my regiment till——" and he stopped short and pointed downwards. He had but one foot; that was why he limped. " Now go back to your inn; I'll settle with the police."

' When we got past the mountains and through Inverness, we were met by two shepherds, sent from John o' Groats to meet us. Our flock by this time were a straggling lot. Instead of moving in one compact mass, they now generally covered some two miles of road, the parties going at speeds according to their strength. One of us with a dog had to walk in front to find the right road ; the other kept the sheep behind on the move. But these two shepherds helped us gloriously, and thirty-six days after we left home we finally delivered our flock to the man who had bought it.

' How did we get home again? John Todd

was a wonderful fast walker, and we made fifty miles a day from John o' Groats down to Carlisle.'

The foregoing remarkable journey was but one of many the old shepherd had made. He had driven sheep to Fortwilliam, at the foot of the Caledonian Canal; had, when Barrow, now a great industrial centre, was a mere village, driven sheep to meet a brig which then plied between Peel Castle and the Isle of Man. The voyage took three days owing to contrary winds, and the poor animals ate every scrap of hay and straw on board the vessel. The shepherd had travelled South as well as North, and knew some of the walks of North and Central Wales well.

Many other stories of his life did he regale me with, but nothing, perhaps, which interested me more than the following curious statement:

'Sheep possess a strong homing instinct on occasion. In the old days, before steam was used for transport, time and again they used to leave the intakes they were bought for and travel many a mile back home again. This was, perhaps, the most remarkable case I ever met with. In the early days of cross-breeding a farmer bought a score of Cheviot tups at one of the Scottish Border towns. A day or two after reaching the farm, they, having been smitted, were put upon the open fell, where they seemed to be quite at home; but before the week-end the shepherd reported every one of the new-comers missing. Every flock ranging the common was searched without success, and the farmer was beginning to fear they had been stolen, when a letter came from the Scottish sheep-walk saying the tups had returned. How they had managed to win home again across the width of three counties, and presumably along the great "drove road," is beyond my comprehension. No doubt this tale is beyond your belief, but I have seen many similar instances, A wandering "stray" is no marvel in a land of shepherds ; but a body of sheep moving in one direction, influenced by a common impulse, which carries them over some sixty miles of intersecting road and through terrifying difficulties (to a sheep), cannot be anything but wonderful.'

II. At a Shepherds' Meet

THE sheep have been collected from the unfenced mountain pastures, and are now being driven down towards the valley for winter. Near the gateway into the enclosed fields the shepherd goes round to the front of the moving flock to let down the bars (or open the gate, as the case may be) for their passage. Two of his dogs are left to drive the sheep downwards, the third accompanying its master. The gate opened, the sheep are allowed to pass singly, while the man posts himself in a position to clearly see the distinctive flock-mark on each animal passing. Should one not show this red or black sign, the nearer dog is signalled, and the animal is rapidly driven to an adjacent fold. After all have passed, the shepherd's attention is turned to these enfolded sheep. The place in which they are standing is divided by a rough wall, and in the largest section the suspects are grouped. Posting a dog in the gap which serves as entrance, the shepherd goes in and examines his 'sorting.' Some are almost irrecognisable wanderers from his own flock, a great many truants from neighbouring heafs, while the remainder belong to adjacent valleys. The sheep of the home dale are shortly driven to their own intakes, and during this round of visits the shepherd receives many of his own 'strays.'

The remaining head cannot easily be returned to farms into the teens of miles away, so to obviate expense the Shepherds' Meet has come into existence. Formerly of great importance, the festival has now fallen to the bare exchange of sheep and an excuse for holiday. The gatherings are usually at places central to a wide area of fells farms ; for example, that held at Mardale attracts the men of that dale, of Swindale and Mosedale, of Bannisdale and Boroughdale, Longsleddale, Kentmere and Troutbeck. There are also famous meets held in Eskdale, Langdale, Wastdale, and at Thirlspot under the shadow of mighty Helvellyn. To these the shepherds of the various districts bring on an appointed day such 'strays' as have not been disposed of, and here come also those who have animals missing from their flocks.

The shepherds working on that great wilderness of mountains between High Street and Fairfield meet at the little whitewashed inn on the summit of Kirkstone Pass. If you are lucky enough to

gain accommodation there on a night in late
November, you will be roused at daybreak by the
quavering plaints of many sheep. Shepherds are
early risers ; as the day is mainly given over to
amusement, they naturally endeavour to get all
business done as early as possible. As you stand
in the roadway, you see many knots of sheep
moving towards the hostelry, in the narrow field
behind which a labyrinth of pens has been con-
structed. As the small flocks pass it, their bleatings
are thrown from the squat white walls of the house
as from an excellent sounding-board, and the steep
ribs of Red Screes echo the sound backward and
forward, fainter each time, till it passes beyond
the ear's perception. In the gray light the scene
around is particularly wild ; above the great rocks
carrion crows are wheeling and sounding their
raucous notes ; in the lofty crag towering to the
left of the great rift in the mountain wall a raven
is croaking and a pair of buzzards skirling.
Nearer at hand, unmoved by the stir and clamour,
dingy sparrows and a few dirty-gray stonechats
are flitting about on their morning business. After
a few minutes passed in the road, comparing this
noisy dawn with last nightfall, when the gray
shades crept from eastward, blotting out distant
mountains and well-like valleys ere darkness
stalked down to this lonely place from the heights,

I turned to where the sheep had been penned. At my elbow was a young farmer of Troutbeck, in search, he said, of five animals which had been missing from his farm since last July.

As the shepherds arrive, their quotas are penned separately, and all around is the buzz of conversation from weather-beaten men, looking intently on each occupant of the rough constructions. Now and again I hear a voice claiming one for his own.

'Ay, this is mine. Looksta at t' blue pop on't nar [near] shoulder?'

'What's yer other marks, Mister Dobson?' says a rugged veteran who seems to have constituted himself steward of this pen.

'Well, noo, I bowt [bought] that fra Jack Briggs o' t' Lilehouse. It'll be horn-marked B on t' right horn, and D on t' left hoof. Hesn't it a "key" in t' right lug [ear]?'

'Ay, Mr. Dobson, it hes.'

The veteran climbs into the pen, and secures the sheep indicated, the loose hurdle is unbound, and Danny walks out with the animal between his legs. A struggling ewe is impossible for me to manage. Hold it as I will, I am dragged hither and thither at its pleasure, and at last am fain to let go ; but these men have mastered the art of control, and in a few seconds the sheep's marks are checked and

it is driven through the rabble of men and dogs
to an empty pen.

The Troutbeck shepherd is standing some yards
away beside a pen containing five half-bred ewes.
As I approach he turns, and remarks, with a
laugh : ' These are mine ! All together, and t'
first lot I've looked at !'

I congratulate him on his luck, then ask him
how he will prove his claim.

' Well, look here '—he vaulted within the enclosure and laid hands on the nearest animal—' all
my sheep are marked with a R burnt on the
horn ; there's t' same on t' hoof, wi' a red stripe
down t' left flank like this. Well, anybody from
our dale knows these marks, and if anyone
doubted me I should bring some of them to
prove it.'

The shepherd and I walked round the strays
still unclaimed ; the wan morning light had
broken into clear day I noticed, but my companion, by his remarks on fells life and customs,
kept my attention closely. Then he suddenly
stopped, and, pointing to a single ewe folded by
itself, he said :

' That sheep 'll not be claimed to-day, I guess.'
Then, turning to the lad in charge, he continued :
' Jimmy, wharriver hesta gitten that fra ?'
[wherever have you got that from ?].

' Why, it com into our flock three week since. Dosta know whar it belongs ?'

' It's a gay way from here. Hesta seen Jimmy Green of Little Langdale about ?'

' He was here five minutes sen. But he can't name it.'

' I'll fetch him ;' and off he went, to return in a minute with a long, lean man of the nervy hunting type. ' Noo, Jim, dosta name it? It belongs to t' priest at Seathwaite. Thoo's handled many a yan [one] o' his when we lived at Tarn Hall together.'

Here followed a technical description of the marks distinguishing the flock of the Vicar of that remote mountain parish, and the upshot was that Green agreed to take the sheep to Little Langdale, till such time as he could spare a day to climb the steep pass of Wrynose, and tramp the seven miles of rough path down the Duddon Valley to where the sheep's owner lived. How had the sheep wandered so far away? I wondered ; the point at which it had been detected was thirty full miles from its rightful home. My companion thought it possible that the ewe had rambled over the fell to some mountain road, and along this had followed in the track of some flock which was being driven from one dale to another. It was likely that one such happening might bring the ewe across all the enclosed ground between two commons, upon the second of which it had been captured.

By this time the business of the meet was over, and mine host called me indoors, and half scoldingly reminded me that the breakfast ordered for seven a.m. remained untouched now, after eight o'clock. My little parlour, I found, had been invaded by a section of the shepherds, a few of whom joined in my meal. I had just got back to the front of the house, when the sound of a hunting horn floated along the stony breast of Red Screes. The stirring notes rose and fell and rose again, dying off at last in a confusion of sweet echoes. A pack of foxhounds is always an attraction at the Kirkstone Meet, and rarely does a good hunt fail them over the splintered seams and lofty slopes which extend for miles on either side. In a few minutes the pack arrived. There were no preliminaries; the huntsmen simply stated that the hounds would operate in a certain direction, and off they went, a knot of stalwart dalesmen in attendance. Up the great hill the quest gradually wound. Every now and again a hound gave tongue, but no scent worth following was discovered. I could see men and hounds scrambling and dodging among the rocks above the first range of cliffs. Suddenly there was a wild chorus; the tiny objects redoubled their speed of ascent. They stood out against the sky-line, a number of slender points, then went out of sight. The huntsman's pink coat had hardly disappeared over the rocky ridge ere another horn heralded the approach of the harriers. These last, with more leisure, cast off in a field just beside the inn, and, more fortunate than the others, had a scent almost at once. I watched them dash away, the hounds outdistancing their followers easily, till a fold of the fell hid them from view.

My interest was less with these sports than with the real business of the meet. Every ten minutes or so a shepherd would start off for his distant home with a few sheep, and I watched each out of sight. I engaged a few men in talk about their calling, but their words were not fluent, and little information could I glean. Then mine host, in a moment of slack business, presented me to a very old man, who, he averred, knew all there was to be known by humans of life on the fells. To this commendation the whole company assented. 'Old Jimmy knows everything about t' old times,' they said.

After a few preliminary questions we got far into the past, and I was surprised to find the old gentleman, at the age of ninety-one, able to give lucid expression to memories of his very young days. He had known Wordsworth, and Professor Wilson of Elleray, and a score more of the great inhabitants of Lakeland. Mr. Ruskin (who at the time was still alive) had on two occasions stayed the night at his house, but of that noble character the old man understood but little.

At this point someone called in from the doorway that the hounds were running in full view. Out we poured in a great hurry, the old man as nimble as any, and moving without the aid even of a stick. We watched the pack gallop hard along the grass, then lost them a moment as they crossed a deep ravine. In less than three minutes the hare led them out of sight again over the ridge, and we saw them no more. The old man elected to tell the remainder of his story in the open air, and, scorning my offer of a chair, sat down on a low wall opposite the inn.

'Now, Kirkstone was not always the place for this Shepherds' Meet. It used to be on the top of Kentmere High Street, a nearly level bit about a mile and a half long. Up there, after the sheep were all exchanged, there used to be horse-racing. You mightn't think a fell pony could get along quickly, but, bless you! they are mighty handy in picking their way across ground covered with stones or peat bogs. Then there used to be a lot of wrestling, with a few foot races and suchlike. Now things are different. When t' meet was first brought to Kirkstone, there used to be a guide's race up to t' top of the fell there,' indicating an almost inaccessible-looking spur of rock and scree; 'but that's been done away with for a bit now. And what wi' hunting both fox and hare, there's no time left for wrestling. Things are altered a deal in every way, and maybe it's as well t' meet changes like other things.'

The old man had many stories which I shall not repeat here. His long life had been spent entirely among the fells, and he was a veritable storehouse of legends and old customs.

The day passed on rapidly, and at evening there was a grand meeting of all the shepherds and followers of both packs. Events were fast settling down to the level of a 'merry night' when I bade mine host farewell and followed the sound of the last departing flock.

III. A Mountain Catastrophe

I WISH it to be clearly understood that I am reproducing, without ornament or argument, the tale of a mountain catastrophe as told by a rheumy little man of sixty-five, the holder of a well-known sheep-farm among the fells. The scene in which it was told to me was one of the bleakest tracts on the Lakeland mountains; others of my party had pushed on towards the dale, leaving me to hear the old man's story. This was told in a strong dialect, reproduced with difficulty in ordinary English, and in this version I have tried to retain the simple directness of his narrative.

*   *   *   *   *

' Joe Sumner was in charge of my sheep in the intake just beyond the pass-head there. In summer I used to go once a week or so to look my lot over, and, with Joe's help, to doctor any sick. In winter I always went up after a snowstorm to help dig out any that had been caught in the drifts. Well, one December there was a fearful storm; the wind from south-east brought eight inches of snow to us in the lowlands. As soon as the worst blew over I harnessed up, took Jim, one of my men, and three dogs, and drove over to Joe's house at the pass-foot. He was waiting for us, and said that he was afraid a good many sheep were lost in a ghyll which had been drifted level. He mounted the trap, bringing a lad to look after the horse while we were in the intakes.

' The way up was pretty bad to drive; here and there the snow had drifted right across the roadway, but the old mare pulled through easily when we had got out and lightened the trap. Just below the summit was about a mile of level nearly clear of drifts, and along this we rattled at a fairish pace. At the top we got out, and sent the lad back with the trap. It had been blowing pretty thin all the morning, but the first sweep into our faces from northward simply doubled us up with cold. The hills around this pass-head always look wild and dreary, but never so bad as when yards deep in snow. Joe and his dogs led us to a hollow in the fellside where in summer a beck rattled down in a score pretty waterfalls. This was drifted nearly level.

' Joe came to a stop at the bottom of this great

mass of snow—a hundred yards long, ten deep, and maybe twenty to thirty wide.

' " I've been out since daylight looking up the sheep, and there's fifty-eight missing—twenty-eight of mine and thirty of yours. My dogs scented a few in Yew-tree Ghyll, and one or two nigh Borwen's Knott, but I hadn't time to dig any of them out. However, I think that the best part of them that is missing are in this ghyll, and maybe we'd better try to get the nearer ones out now."

'A pair of spades were going very shortly in an outlying patch, where the dogs had marked a buried sheep. The snow was dry, and flew in great clouds like powder. I was watching the others at work. The breeze was—well, I said its first sweep was a marvel for coldness, and I thought it wasn't possible for wind to be more bitter. But as the minutes went on, it grew decidedly worse, so I took shelter behind a big rock. Of course, a wind could hardly blow over many a weary mile of snow and then be anything but freezing itself. I whistled for the dogs, but they didn't come, and in a few minutes, wondering what mischief they were up to, I ventured out. Was that old Dobbin ranging on the road half a mile away? I whistled my hardest—dogs can pick up a further sound than a man, as any shepherd knows: it stopped a moment, then turned and leathered heedlessly away. Black, Nan, and Bob were also on the road galloping for home. I couldn't understand it, so called Joe up. He was puzzled as well.

'"There's something in it," he said, pondering like, as he looked around. "I bet it's fairly frozen the poor little beggars out. Whew! I never knew it so cold as this, even on the pass!"

'We were both looking northwards towards the dark lake and the dismal white mountains, when the great mass of a far-off range suddenly disappeared, and in its place a murky gray cloud seemed to leap from summit to summit in our direction. Joe gasped, and then turned with a yell:

'"Jim, come on sharp! There's a regular host of a storm coming. Now, mister, ye'll have to step lively if we're to be over the pass before that great whirlwind of snow catches us!"

'Down the snow-slope we ran, but we had barely reached the track before the gale was on us so strong we could hardly keep our feet. Beside which the snow whirled down so thick that we could hardly see one another even between the gusts.

'I heard Joe's voice yell above the storm,

"Keep close to me, both of you!" I did my utmost, but as we got on to the plain [bleak] pass-head, with a wild skirl the wind got hold of me, and threw me headforemost into a deep drift. I'm not thinking you'll believe me, but I had a fearful job getting out of that. The wind seemed almost solid with pelting snow, and every time I staggered to my knees it knocked me flat again.

'In a few minutes I managed, in a lull between two earth-shaking blasts, to get on to my feet and make a rush for the road, which, at least, was free of snow. Then, jumping up as each gust blew over, and running in the little quiet before another came along, I got to the top of the pass and down into a fairly sheltered cove. Here Jim and Joe hailed me with delight. They were wondering how I had come on, Joe holding that I was all right, and the other being equally sure that some big drift had got me. *They* had been knocked flat by the gust that almost buried me, after which, taking advantage of every slack in the storm, they had got to shelter a good ten minutes earlier.

'After this we got down to Joe's house and waited—the sheep must stick [stay] for the present. The dogs, coming in long before we did, had put the folks out terribly.

'It was near midnight when the snow passed

off and we made a new start. This time our aim was not so much to dig out the lost ones, as to collect and drive down every sheep we could find. It was bright moonlight when we set off; the air was still, and the stars glished [gleamed] down as bright as if they were but a mile away. Have you ever been on a pass-head with mountains all around on a moonlight night ? Some folks call it sublime and awesome, but those words mean nothing to plain men like me. Three of us climbing through drifts and along stony roads felt like we did when we were bairns, and ventured alone after dark where we believed ghosts and fairies lived. We used to cower along as if at every step we expected something terrible to happen, with our shoulders drawn in, waiting for a heavy hand to strike us. I remember well my half-sobs and nervous looks around when I had to cross the wood beyond the stepping-stones, where a murder once took place. This time we didn't sob, though our other feelings were the same.

'On the pass-head everything was so still that it was quite a relief when Joe whistled his dogs away to the top end of the intake, where a crowd of dark gray dots could be seen on the white. I sent my dogs to watch the further side, keeping them near the places where drifts had buried the fences. Our shouts and whistles seemed strangled in our throats by that queer stillness; but, still, they must have travelled well, for the dogs made never a mistake. The air was cold, freezing cold, but it was still, and the chill was nothing compared to the searching bite of the wind earlier in the day. In about half an hour a mixed flock of my sheep and Joe's were being brought with loud bleatings down to where we stood.

'Our return down the pass was done in darkness—if the combined shining of stars, northern lights, and the reflection off miles of snow, is darkness—after which I should have been glad to get to bed awhile. But Joe was determined that the sheep must be dug for at once; the great hollow where most of them lay would fill with water if a sudden thaw came, and any sheep then left in would surely be suffocated. He went the round of his neighbours' farms to pick up any men that could be spared, while I sent the trap home for what servants my place could do without. Collecting workers is always a tedious job, but in four hours we had nine spademen mustered, and made a move for the third time up the drifted track.

'Gray dawn was just coming when we got to the top of the pass; the silence of moonlight was gone, and our company's talk made the dreary hillsides echo. We had plenty of dogs, so a few of us went to Borwen's Knott—a stiff climb, where every few minutes we seemed to slip back as far as we had dragged forward. My back ached long before we got to where the sheep had been marked, and I lagged behind to rest. When I got up to the others, the dogs had marked down three sheep at no great depth—perhaps a yard or so—and the spades were clearing the snow away like mad. In a minute or two the sheep were clear, and we sent them off towards the pass-road. One of the dogs scented another close in under the crags of the Knott, and to get this out seemed like to give a lot of work. How do these sheep get buried, you say? Well, it's sheep nature when a storm—wind, snow, rain, or the three together —gets to a certain pitch to lie down with their backs toward it. Like that they bide [remain] till the worst is over, no matter whether they are buried overhead or not. For a sheep can breathe easily through a covering of twenty feet of snow; and as its body-heat thaws a little cave, the weight above, though it may be tons, doesn't harm it at all. The breathing-places on the snow can be picked out by a man if the sheep aren't far under; but if they are, it takes a dog all its time to find where the beast lies. Now, as I was saying, these lost sheep at Borwen's Knott were right in among the rocks, and pretty deep down. The shepherds, however, dug a deep trench in the drift which had plastered itself against the Knott, and after an hour's hard work the sheep jumped up not a bit worse. At Yew-tree Ghyll a gang got down to the sheep without much trouble; one of them was so lively after passing thirty hours or more in a drift that it butted over three of the shepherds in making for the open.

'Joe reckoned that twenty-four sheep were in the deepest part of the big ghyll, and that another score could be got at in a day's work. While the spades were beginning work, I and two of my men took our dogs and went over the whole two intakes thoroughly. At one spot we had a surprise. A hollow in the hillside not more than a yard deep had been drifted level, and in this were, maybe, a dozen rounded lumps — tops of rocks covered with snow, we thought; but my man Jackson, as we crossed the flat, kicked his foot against one, and found nothing hard. He stopped to examine the thing. It was a sheep, lying just as it had turned its back to the storm, not covered with more than a foot of snow. We whistled the dogs up, and as they came floundering along, fully a dozen ewes jumped up and made away.

'"Ho, ho!" said I, "this find 'll make Joe Sumner stare. He'll have to alter his figures as to what's in that great ghyll if we go on like this."

' But though we found no other great number, a careful look about the walls and other likely places showed us where more lay. Altogether, our tramp about the intakes brought up twenty-three ewes in good strength and condition. One poor thing we found with a leg broken by a stone which somehow had split from the side of a rough outcrop, and another was in the pool beneath a force in the beck that runs into the valley, drowned. Joe Sumner was surprised at how we had come on. A dozen men working for their lives fairly in that great pile of snow in the beck-course had got three sheep out in as many hours. But their digging was coming near to a flat grassy spot where a dozen or so sheep lay, and here all expected success. And it was not long in coming. The sheep had clustered almost into one mass, and were lifted out one after another. In their haste the spademen had left the snow overhanging some four or five feet, and just as the seventh sheep was lugged [hauled] out, a big patch gave way, smothering everything for two or three minutes in a cloud of whirling snow-dust. When this cleared somewhat, it was found that two shepherds were still under the snow. Spades had been used before at some speed, but I can tell you *that* was nothing to the rush put on now. For what's the price of a sheep to the value of the life of a man? Tons of snow were whirled aside, and in five minutes the first man was reached. He had an ugly gash on the side of his head : he had been driven down with tremendous force on to the blade of his spade. But he was still conscious, and reiterated weakly what we knew too well: " Jack Howson was further in nor [than] me."

'The spademen stopped work not a moment ; for though a sheep can breathe through many feet of snow, a man suffers terribly when buried over a foot. Soon a boot was reached, and in a few seconds the drift had been thrown aside sufficiently for Howson to be lifted out. He was pretty much dazed, but no worse for the mishap, and in ten minutes he again took his share of the digging. Immediately beneath where his body had been lying an old ewe was found, and seven more within some two yards. Altogether, thirteen sheep were brought out. Only five were missing from both flocks now—three from mine and two from Joe's ; and as we couldn't find the exact places — the snow was so deep that the dogs couldn't scent them—where they were lying, we were forced to let them bide [remain]. They might have the luck, we thought, to live through till the thaw came, and the melting snow mightn't, perhaps, drown them all. Besides '—and here the native shrewdness of the shepherd shone through the eloquence of the raconteur—' it would have cost a deal to dig the ghyll clear of snow—far more than five ewes at forty shillings apiece are worth.'

Seemingly, with this the story was ended, but I queried what eventually became of the five missing sheep.

'All lost in the thaw,' was the reply. 'The beck flooded, and the drift sucked the water in till they were suffocated, poor things!'

IV. In Wild Weather

UNDER its canopy of leafless sycamores the sheep-farm stands high above the next most remote dwelling in the dale. It is a pleasant place to dwell in during summer: the great fells clothed with green, spreading beds of bracken rise close around. A great rib of rock and scree almost cuts off the tenement, so that it commands only a narrow view of the long, almost level valley. But, though so close confining it, the mountain protects neither the buildings nor the farm land immediately adjoining from the fury of winter storms. When the air becomes filled with sleet, the fields and rough mountain roads stand mid-leg-deep with half-liquid snow. A hundred feet above, the clouds fly in dense ragged beards; their damp breath penetrates nigh even to the cosy kitchen fire. The scene is cheerless: gray sky and grayer dale, relieved only with white where in the shelter of the rocks a small snowdrift resists the general thaw, or where in foamy spouting cataracts the flooded becks are gushing. Dimly seen through the sheets of snow and rain, the sheep are cowering in the dips of the intakes, and among them the shepherd is moving.

As he returns to the steading for another load of hay—it were cruelty indeed to expose even the hardiest horse to the terrible 'clash' prevailing—I walk out to intercept him.

'Can I help you?' I ask.

For a moment he surveys my outfit of mackintosh, leggings, and multifarious wraps ; apparently I pass muster, for he says quite kindly:

'Well, if you like ; but it *does* blow something cruel outside of the fold. You had better go back to the kitchen.'

This put me on my mettle, and I declined to retire. Without another word, the shepherd slung a rope round a big bundle of hay, and helped me with it on my shoulders.

'Can you manage it?' he asked.

It was barely possible, but I would not admit it, especially as he, a spare, bent figure of a man little more than half my size, was already shouldering a bundle of about double the weight. My load seemed to spread over my neck and head, driving my chin perforce on to my chest, and causing me to breathe with increasing difficulty.

'Now follow me,' said Ralph, as he staggered

through the wide doorway. Clear of the buildings the storm was raging more wildly. A heavy gust, almost solid with sleet, struck us, and at its onslaught I reeled against a convenient wall. When my eyes, dashed with water, took service again, I saw Ralph stepping ahead over the sloppy fold. The mountain of hay he was almost buried in proved a good point to guide by, though the start he had obtained while the gust held me prisoner gradually increased till it became difficult to see him through the films of falling rain. The fold-gate reached—Ralph had propped it ajar—a bleating throng encompassed me.

'Where shall I drop it?' I called, my attention being for a moment diverted from my companion, and from a long way in advance his voice replied:

'Come on! it is for the ewes by the beckside.'

To reach this point we had to face a short ascent and cross a tiny exposed level. This was the very vortex of the hurricane. No sooner had I stepped on to it than the powerful gusts hustled me round and round, dragged my load from my shoulders, and threw it yards away, depositing me meanwhile in a deep basin of snow-broth. The great dashing curtains of snow and rain and this mishap completely wet me though. It therefore seemed of little avail to abandon the job, so I looked round for Ralph. He was delivering his forage to a crowd of pushing sheep two hundred yards away. I essayed unaided to lift the bundle in my charge, but not until the third attempt did it consent to balance on my shoulders. I now made a quick rush in Ralph's direction. My feet were far from as sure as Ralph the shepherd's on such slippery ground. The storm tumbled and tossed me about; my unwieldy bundle, caught by the wind, whirled me bodily away, spun me round, then whisked me off my feet entirely. In ten minutes, and after three attempts, I got nearly three-quarters of my journey over, but so storm-tossed that I had to signal the waiting shepherd to come to my aid. He carried the bundle the rest of the way.

For a moment the wild screeching of the gale among the crags above ceased. The sheep crowded round us, intent on getting their share of the forage. Poor miserable creatures they looked, for in winter these valley lands are at best unhealthy. The little corner Ralph had selected for a feeding-place was somewhat sheltered from the sweep of the storm, but the flock had trodden the ground into a perfect quagmire, from which they were now picking stray wisps of muddied hay.

'Well,' said Ralph, 'what do you think of them?'

I had to say that the sheep did not seem very

first-class, to which the shepherd replied that there was hardly a flock in the dale in better condition. Fell sheep are brought down from the highest ground in November, and many are sent on to the marshlands near the sea for winterage. As this means certain expense, however, the farmer must in these hard days keep as many sheep at home as he possibly can. Should a protracted season of frost and snow ensue, the slender resources of hay and roots are soon exhausted, and then there is much suffering for the flock. Ralph seemed to feel the misery of his flock as much as any of its individual members.

'But,' said the shepherd, 'our sheep aren't as bad as they used to be in my grandfather's time. He says that frequently nearly one-half of the lambs never went to heaf again after winter. Footrot and lungworm used to kill them by scores. Now let us walk round the intake, and see how the others are faring. I fed them up at the top end before it was light this morning, and I wasn't sure all the sheep turned up.'

Though the storm bellowed and hurled its forces against us, we struggled round that great enclosure. Even on the most exposed shoulder, in every cranny among the rocks, in every fold in the hill where there was anything like shelter, in every beck-course, there were sheep. Back-turned to the seething gale, silent, mournfully chewing their cud. Said Ralph the shepherd :

' It makes my heart bleed to see them like this, but, then, what can I do?'

One sheep, after careful numbering, was missing, and after a long search we found it. It had been wandering along the edge of the stream, and had fallen down the steep bank into the water. One leg was broken by the fall ; it was one of the most ailing of the flock, so weak that it had drowned in a very small pool.

Our patrol over, I returned to the farm kitchen. How cosy a fire looks to one who has been struggling against chill and damp furies for three or four hours ! My return was hailed with a chorus of protests against ever turning out on such a day ; but I had seen something of the most unpleasant and fatiguing side of shepherd-life, which I could not fail to remember.

Twenty minutes later Ralph left the kitchen to recommence his duties ; but flesh and spirit were alike weak, and I did not then accompany him. Till darkness fell, I watched from the inside of a stout home the day's mood vary from whirling snow to thundering gale and to clashing curtains of rain ; then, as night really began, we drew fire-wards.

'Where's Ralph? Hesn't he come in yet?' asked the old farmer from the depths of his chair.

'He's just gone round to let his dogs out,' was the reply. 'He says there's some sheep want driving in a bit for the night.'

At this the shepherd himself opened the door. He was dripping wet, but that was what he had been all day, and in his eyes lived tiredness.

'Will some of you come and give me a hand with the sheep from the top end? I'll have to have them nearer if they're to be looked at again to-night.'

Three of us promptly offered our services. Lanterns were brought, and soon we started. Even with our lights not more than ten yards could be seen. Soon I lost touch with the others, and for an hour wandered about the storm-swept fellside. Then in the lulls I began to hear men and dogs and sheep on the move: the others were bringing the flock towards the farm. These men had had an exciting time; snow-fringed ghylls and slippery rock-faces had provided real dangers to avoid.

Home at last! The wearied Ralph, divesting himself of several layers of outer garments, went off to bed. We leisured ones sat by the fireside awhile, yarning of fox and sheep and dog and bird—the sport and work of a mountain farm.

The winter dragged on to its weary close. Many days of tempest came, and were calmly endured. When the weather allowed it, we wandered after sport : sometimes a pack of foxhounds was in the vicinity, or the guns were brought out for a shot at migratory wild-fowl. February ended in genial weather, and for a few days of March it continued. After this came an ominous gradual change in the weather.

For a fortnight or so the bitter east winds raged among the mountains and hissed into the dalehead through the narrow passes. But this was seasonable. In a few more days these fierce blasts would exhaust themselves, and more genial weather follow. But, instead of clearing away, the clouds, our constant companions during the long drear winter, crept further down the rugged braes, and occasional snowflakes hovered in the air. In those scant moments when the gale whirled the beleaguering gray masses aside and showed the uplands, we could see that snow-squalls had been frequent. The glasses at the farm portended unsettled weather, and in the Beck Hause flocks lambs were beginning to come. For three days every hand, in varying degrees of efficiency, had been working restlessly, almost frantically, tending the sheep and the newly-arrived lambs. It was impossible to provide shelter for the two thousand sheep on the holding, so the ewes likely to lamb within the next three days were driven into the most sheltered intake—a bleak place at best in this 'snerping' wind.

At mid-day the white fury whirled down; the strong sunshine of spring was cut off by the advancing storm, and we were groping in semi-darkness. So dense were the snow-wreaths that no further than ten yards could be seen at any time, and long ere sunset the ancient horn lanterns were being used by the shepherds. When struck by a storm, sheep generally get to the cover of the nearest wall or bed of boulders, and to this trait we owed much during the hours of stress which now followed.

A succession of patrols went round the intakes, in which ewes and lambs were huddling in scanty shelter. The storm grew wilder; the snow lay inches deep. I had charge of a small hovel among the farm buildings, where a score of ewes which had already lambed had been driven. So intensely nervous is the average sheep that a light had to be kept burning in the shed, and I had to accustom them to my presence. If my candles had blown out, I was assured that every sheep, in her anxiety, would have endeavoured to 'mother' her lambs close to her, with the result that in the confusion most of them would have been trampled upon. Now and again a panic would begin. The sheep, restlessly moving about, would break into plaintive bleatings; but at a word they would be pacified, and relapse into silent suffering. At about midnight the door was opened, and one of the maid-servants relieved me. No one would go to bed till the storm had spent its violence. The gale outside was fearful, and I was badly thrown about in my attempt to cross the few yards to the kitchen door. The other females of the house were busy trying to persuade two little lambs which were lying on the hearthrug to drink some cow's milk. These poor things were orphans of an hour, for their mother had died from exposure soon after giving them birth. The shepherd had picked the unfortunate little mites up, covered them with his greatcoat, and carried them gently to the warmth and care of the kitchen. I asked casually where the other shepherd was. No one had seen him since he set out, four hours ago, to look over the flock outside the lambing intake. 'Maybe he had come across some ewes lambing which hadn't been expected yet.' After swallowing some supper—I was hungry, else the heat and stench of the hovel I had just left would have destroyed my appetite —I went into the hall to glance at the glass.

The storm still continued, and I prepared to go with Jack the shepherd through the lambing intake. Lanterns and dry coats were ready for us —you live in leggings on a farm some thirteen hundred feet above sea-level in winter—and soon we were outside. The blizzard beat into our faces as we groped across the fold to the gateway. Immediately we passed this, Jack pulled my sleeve, indicating that we should go right ahead. It was no use speaking, for the loudest human voice would have been lost in the storm-clamour. The lambing intake was about one-third of a mile long, on the 'lown'd,' or leeward, side of the valley, and the sheep were on the farther side.

We had almost got across the space in the face of the howling tempest, when Jack, taking advantage of a momentary cessation of the gale, shouted: 'We'd better go up this ghyll—there's likely one or two in it.' Accordingly, we plunged into a drift-bounded hollow, and, peering to right and left as far as the feeble rays of our lantern gave light, gradually ascended it. But not a fleece could we discover; some of the snow-banks, indeed, were deep enough to have overwhelmed a flock. At last the shepherd turned his glimmer of light on to a rounded hummock in the spreading white. Something told his practised eye that a sheep was lying here under the lee of a big boulder (the rounded hummock), and in a few seconds we disentombed it. The snow was only a few inches thick, but the ewe's position was one of great danger. We quietly drove it to the shelter of the wall.

We had walked down some way before we came upon other sheep, and here was one which had just lambed. The poor little creatures were lying on the freezing snow-crust, while their mother made frantic efforts in her weak condition to lick them dry. If a lamb is exposed to severe cold for even a short time at this stage of existence, it never recovers. The shepherd forced the lambs to swallow a little milk, and in a while they were standing upright and out of immediate danger. As we followed down the wall the sheep seemed to know us, and watched us come and go without terror. Perhaps they found some company on that wild night in the periodic lantern visits. Towards three a.m., wet through with the sleet and mist, with hands almost frozen, we returned to the farmstead, to be told that the other shepherd had not yet come in, and that some harm might have befallen him. Though the wind was shrieking over the pitch-dark dale, and the cold was, seemingly, more intense; though the snow-blizzard had gradually developed into an awful sleet, and the snow-wreaths were piled high—it was no time to draw back, to wait for help and daylight. The shepherd's favourite dog was brought out, and three of us tramped sorely and wearily back into the darkness. For awhile we beat the boundaries of the intake closely, visiting every corner where a sheep might have been lying, without avail. Then, as we passed a narrow gully, the old dog gave a sign for which we had been looking. In a few minutes we had located the portion of drift in which Ralph was lying, and ere long we saw a portion of cloth in the excavation we made. A couple of minutes later we were carrying the senseless body towards the farm.

When he recovered consciousness, the shepherd stated that he had looked over the sheep in the further intake, and was returning, when his footing on the snow gave way and he was hurled some little distance down. At the end of his fall his head struck against something hard, and he immediately lost consciousness. The next thing he remembered was being 'brought round' in the farm kitchen. Of course, it was Providential that we commenced the search so opportunely, but our best efforts would have been in vain had not the good old dog given us the right direction in which to dig.

The night dragged on wearily. Long ere daybreak we were all tired out, but our task was too important to be allowed to lapse. A few more lambs were born, some to die from their exposure, whilst others were saved. With the first glimpse of coming day the sleet gave way to cold, pelting rain. In a very short time the white garb of the dale had turned a sloppy discolour, and we were splashing about through knee-deep slush. By ten a.m. the thaw had apparently well set, and the mountain torrents began to make their voices heard through the quieting gale. We had some anxious moments searching the ghylls down which floods were beginning to surge; count and patrol as we would, a score sheep could not be accounted for, and it was very possible that they were in some of the numerous gullies. The way in which the rising streams soaked and lapped over the drifts which here and there had formed in their courses was sufficiently suggestive of the fate of any ewe therein entombed. The dogs—the shepherd's only resource—were quickly brought out, and before long spades were being wielded in one or two of the ghylls. At one point the dogs stopped on the level, wet snow-fields. 'Bruce Ghyll!' muttered one of the shepherds. A week previously we had scrambled up this narrow ravine, but now there was no sign of it. However, we began to dig, and in a while had uncovered three sheep—two alive, and one smothered in the sodden

drift. The dogs gave no further attention to the
snow, so we moved on, and in a few minutes were
standing by the edge of a tiny fold in the steep
hillside. Here was a small basin, some two score
yards in width, and maybe a yard and a half deep,
but level with drifted snow. The three dogs ran
over the surface, giving deep barks as they came
opposite where a sheep was buried and scratched
the surface. In the drift were our remaining
' missing '—all safe, and not far beneath the
surface. We had hardly got them released before
the wind shouted an angry warning from the
mountains, followed by a tremendous snow-squall,
during the passage of which it was difficult to
stand upright. When this had spent itself, and
was being followed by a downpour of rain, we got
back to the farmhouse. The damage done by the
storm so far was twenty-nine lambs and seven
ewes dead. Had our lambing season been more
advanced, Beck Hause, from its great altitude
and bleak aspect, would have suffered terribly.

'FELL-WALKING' RECORDS

'FELL-WALKING' RECORDS

THIS chapter may be described as a collection of the ' fell-walking ' records of Lakeland, with as much comparison in fact and figure as may interest the general reader. They are not competitive events in accordance with the common use of the word 'record'; but primarily, at all events, were carried out that men might look back in after-years to the time when they were strong and active, and could climb mountain after mountain.

As a comparison of the walking and climbing powers of the men to be mentioned, no account can be absolutely accurate. No two parties take precisely the same routes in their walks, each avoiding some particular variety of fell-land—scree, boulder, crag, or bog—and the value of these avoidances varies in the estimates of other men. The admixture of road and fell over which these walks have been taken is unfavourable to exactitude, for a point-to-point record, involving a considerable stretch of level, may not really be so gigantic a task as a twenty-four hours' walk over fells exclusively. Another element which cannot be resolved into figures is the weather, which, as in all outdoor events, is an important factor towards success. An unexpected snow-squall, a freezing gale, or a dense mist, may completely stop a walk; whereas on bright, cool days, with dry surfaces underfoot, great distances are compassed with ease.

In this comparison a few rules with regard to figures have been more or less followed, but circumstances often make any systematic treatment useless. While miles walked on the road may be classed as units, the fatigue of each mile over mountain-land varies considerably. According to one eminent authority, the average fell mile is equal to two by road. When screes or boulders are negotiated, each mile will be more difficult; while when great ascents are climbed, the unit may equal as many as four ordinary miles. The energy required in crossing grassy moors, on the other hand, may not be more than equal to road work, but is best assessed as ranging from one and one-eighth to one and a half, according to slope and climatic conditions. Boggy stretches, how-ever, make sport with figures—after a wet period their passing is often as exhausting as the hardest ascents; in dry times they are quite easily dealt with. The in-and-out nature of the figures quoted below must be attributed to such accidentals as these. When record making, some men take all favourable slopes at a run, and this mode of progression is very wearying, though the rapid waste of power may not be noticed at the time. Others, to save too severe concussion of foot and leg muscles, walk down such places, when the fatigue mileage must be only increased by one-half to compensate.

In general, ' fell walks ' resolve themselves into two classes, the first including attempts to pass a specified number of points in the shortest possible time ; the second, records in which the time only is approximately fixed. It must also be remembered that these long walks only attract a few men in a generation, and whole decades have passed without anything noteworthy being done. During the past few seasons more than usual attention has been given to the sport, and it is to be hoped that still greater interest will be aroused.

A fell walk calls for more than speed and strength ; vigilance of eye and foot must combine to cope with the ever-changing level. There must be a certain ' hold-back ' of power to change, as a flash, stride into leap, walk into run. The ability to journey accurately through damp mist ; the strength and endurance to cope with the sterner side of the weather; the precise knowledge of locality; the instant recognition of the faintest landmark or sign of Nature, and its application to rectify any error—without these a long fell walk cannot be carried out.

Then, of course, a man must be trained to the task—that is, if he is to do it with the greatest possible ease. Few of the men who have done these enormous walks could be termed 'trained,' by any stretch of the imagination. This form of athleticism is different from any other popular sport, and the training requisite is therefore of a different kind. The man must not be too finely drawn, as a good deal of 'substance' is required. A fell walker is constantly jolting himself as he copes with the ground, leaping here, balancing himself on a rock pinnacle there, and unless there was a considerable reserve force no man would be equal to the task.

All the fell-walking records have been made over three great mountain groups: Skiddaw, lying to the north of the Greta, including the peaks of Skiddaw (3,054 feet) and Saddleback or Blencathra (2,847 feet). About twelve miles south of this is the Scawfell range, the backbone of the Lake District, lying at the heads of Borrowdale, Langdale, Wastdale, and Eskdale, and comprising three main peaks—Scawfell (3,163 feet), Scawfell

Pike (3,208 feet), and Great End (2,984 feet). These are divided by Eskhause from the Bowfell Chain (2,960 feet), and by the Styehead Pass from Great Gable (2,949 feet) and its kindred giants. This district contains the roughest and highest ground in England ; in fact, its rocky slopes afford the crag-climbing which has given the Lake District a name for such work. Helvellyn is the remaining mountain mass, divided from the Scawfell group by a long moor, some 1,800 feet in average altitude, and nine miles in breadth, and from the Skiddaw group by the vale of the Glenderamakin. It divides the Thirlmere and Legburthwaite valleys from Patterdale and Grasmere, its chief peaks being Helvellyn (3,118 feet), and Fairfield (2,863 feet) across the Grisedale Tarn depression. The rest of the country is furrowed into deep, narrow valleys.

The pioneer in ' record walking ' was the Rev. T. M. Elliott, of Cambridge, who in the early sixties made the round of the fells surrounding Wastdalehead. After scaling Scawfell, he passed over Scawfell Pike and Great End into the Styehead Pass. From here he climbed the Great Gable, whence, keeping on the highest ground, he walked, by way of Kirkfell, the Pillar Mountain, and the Steeple, to Red Pike and Stirrup Crag, finishing at Wastdalehead. His time was eight and a half hours, during which 6,500 feet were ascended, and a round of some fifteen miles covered, requiring energy sufficient for thirty-eight level miles. Practically all the walking was done on ground more elevated than 1,500 feet. Mr. Elliott, who did much Alpine climbing, met his death by falling from a glacier, July, 1869.

In the spring of 1870 a notable walk was performed by Mr. Thomas Watson, of Darlington, and Wilson, the Lodore guide. For the height ascended, the distance covered, and the rapidity with which it was executed, this excursion ranks high. The pair left Keswick just before midnight, and covered the nine miles to Seathwaite by 2 a.m., thence making for Scawfell Pike, where they were greeted by a most unwelcome snowsquall. They next wended their way through Langdalehead, and across the Stake Pass to Wythburn and Helvellyn, where, the mist being very dense, they more than once lost their way. During a most unfavourable evening they ascended Saddleback and Skiddaw, the strong wind over the forest compelling them to progress over the more exposed portions on hands and knees. The walk was concluded at 7.45 p.m., and in figures works out to—Total elevation, 10,507 feet; time, 20¾ hours; distance in miles, 48; equivalent on the level, 74 miles.

Again for several years no fresh record was made, till a well-known member of the Alpine Club tried to climb Bowfell, Scawfell Pike, Helvellyn, and Skiddaw in one day. Accompanied by old Mackereth, the Langdale guide, he barely succeeded. His general course has been adopted as the 'four fells record' of later climbers. The total distance was forty-one miles, of which sixteen and a half were over the fells. In fatigue the route was equivalent to fifty-seven miles level. The total of elevation reached 9,000 feet.

The first successful attempt to cut this was by the brothers Tucker, in June, 1878. They left Elterwater at 4.20 a.m., and reached the summit of Bowfell in the remarkable time of one hour forty minutes. The day now developed extreme heat, the thermometer reaching 78° in the shade. Passing over the rough crags to Eskhause, they scaled Scawfell Pike by 8 a.m., and then began the long descent into Borrowdale and to Keswick. At two o'clock the four were standing on the top of Skiddaw—a very fast performance, averaging four and a half miles per hour on the road, and just over two on the fell. This speed was too good to last, and Helvellyn, some fifteen miles away over fairly even ground, took six hours to reach, but this period included refreshments. Getting their second strength, the long descent to Grasmere was soon reached, whence a couple of miles over Red Bank would have finished the route. But, as the brothers elected to walk home by way of Rydal and Ambleside, the record route received an addition of ten miles, Elterwater not being reached till 11.58 p.m. The total time was nineteen hours thirty-eight minutes, and the pace over the whole approached three miles per hour. The four brothers—one of whom is now Bishop of Uganda, and another a well-known landscape artist—were fine lusty men, hardened to the fell, and renowned walkers.

The above figures represented the record until August, 1895, when Messrs. Dawson, Poole, and Palmer made an attempt. At 1 a.m. on a wet morning Mr. J. J. Astley started the party from Elterwater Common. The clouds were soon climbed into, and then commenced the grope upwards. Bowfell caërn was reached by 3.20 a.m., fully forty-five minutes behind the record, after which the trio made for Eskhause. At no period was a greater distance than a hundred yards clear, and consequently the path was soon lost. The rugged beauty of the crags in Ewer Gap, with the dark brooding Angle Tarn beneath, may be appreciated in broad daylight; but when torrents of rain and the coldness of the hour before dawn are added, the scene becomes dreadful rather than sublime. At one stage the party came to a very steep declivity, and were preparing to descend, when a whirl of wind sent the mist clear from below. There, at the foot of a precipice, on the brink of which the three stood, was Angle Tarn; an advance of a few more yards would have put them in a precarious position. With Eskhause lighter banks of mist were reached, and the less pronounced darkness pointed to sunrise. Palmer, who had injured his knee in crossing one of the crag-beds, now began to move with difficulty, and within five minutes of Scawfell Pike gave up the attempt. This peak was reached by 5.5 a.m., and forty-five minutes later the party divided on Eskhause, Dawson and Poole continuing through Borrowdale to Skiddaw. In the valley the sun came out splendidly, but the tops did not clear all day. Skiddaw was climbed by 11.15 a.m., thirty-five minutes in arrears. Being behind at this stage of the walk did not promise much success, but it was hoped that time would be gained towards Helvellyn, and so it proved. This last point was made at 4 p.m., with twenty minutes in hand, the descent, being varied toward Dunmail Raise, enabling the walkers to reach the Traveller's Rest, near Grasmere, at 5.53. Palmer, who had crossed from Elterwater, here met the pair, and, despite his condition, paced his comrades to the end.

Ambleside was passed at 7.22, and the walk came
to a finish, amid general enthusiasm, at 8.17¾ p.m.,
the record thus being improved by twenty and a
quarter minutes. It was really a technical victory,
but, considering the calibre of the climbers, a
wonderful one. The 1895 party did not know
much of the ground, Palmer being the only one
who knew anything of the route between Scawfell
and Helvellyn, and his early retirement probably
hindered the result.

A great climber, of whom I shall have much
to say later, Mr. R. W. Broadrick, next
attacked the record. He was far superior to
any of his predecessors, and was able to pick a
good day for the walk. On April 27, 1900, he
started from Ambleside at 4.20 a.m., reaching
Bowfell two hours thirty-nine minutes later.
Scawfell Pike was passed at 7.55, and Skiddaw
at 12.24. At the foot of this mountain Mr.
Broadrick left his purse by a stream where he had
a slight meal, and lost forty-five minutes in going
back for it. Helvellyn was ascended before five
o'clock, and the whole journey was made in fifteen
hours twenty-six minutes.

It is not surprising to find that the most
appreciated record is the twenty-four hours, and
several attempts on it may be instanced. Only
such as can be verified are chronicled ; many feats

passed down in gossip must be ignored. Routes are more varied in these climbs than in the 'points' records, some climbers, owing to bad weather at the time of their attempt, skirting mountains which others have ascended, or taking them at different points.

The first long walk of which cognizance can be taken was carried out in the seventies by Mr. Charles Pilkington, President of the Alpine Club, and his cousins, who started from Lodore at 11 p.m. They climbed Great Gable, but, dense mist descending, the walk was abandoned for half an hour. Later the morning promised something better, so they climbed by Sprinkling Tarn to Eskhause, and over Scawfell Pike and Great End. Returning from this détour, Mat Barnes, the guide, not relishing the heavy clouds on Hanging Knott, led down to Angle Tarn, where a steep path leads direct to Bowfell Top. The difficult return negotiated, the party made for Dunmail Raise, and struggled along a rough path over the shoulder of Seat Sandal to Fairfield, a peak across Tongue Ghyll. Mr. Pilkington then dropped for Grisedale Tarn down a series of screes, the longest in the Lake District. The mist thinning to some extent, Helvellyn was next climbed, then Saddleback and Skiddaw, Lodore being reached by 11.25, the whole tour occupying twenty-four hours and twenty-five minutes, with a very punishing finish, as the party wished to get in within the twenty-four hours. Mr. Pilkington's party was exceptionally unfortunate in having so much mist to contend with during the day, as otherwise they would have easily finished in the specified time. The total of height ascended was 13,792 feet, and the distance runs to sixty miles, with a fatigue equivalent of eighty miles level.

Next to this performance came a famous walk. On June 17, 1876, Mr. Jenkinson—who afterwards compiled a splendid guide-book to the Lakes—did a remarkable walk. He was a man of middle height, sturdily built, and a grand walker. His action on the level was easy, while his dexterity among screes and boulders was something to marvel at. Mr. Jenkinson left Keswick at twelve midnight—a lovely night with bright starlight—and soon after 3 a.m. was standing at Styehead Tarn, with Great Gable looming over him. To the top of this (from the tarn a climb of 1,519 feet) and back again occupied little over an hour, after which he took the path for Eskhause and Scawfell Pike. Before 7.30 he was on the highest ground in England. The mist, which had for awhile threatened to descend, became dense, and for three hours the famous walker wandered round Eskhause, endeavouring to reach

Bowfell by way of Hanging Knott. Just before 11 a.m. he reached the summit, after which the steep descent into Langdale Fellhead prepared him for a tramp to Wythburn. After about an hour's stay at this village he climbed Helvellyn, and, by way of the Vale of St. John, Saddleback. From here he crossed Skiddaw Forest, but could hardly keep up for sleepiness. At a gamekeeper's house he rested awhile, and, naturally, resumed his walk sleepier than ever. The summit of Skiddaw Mr. Jenkinson never had more than a hazy idea of scaling—he often joked that he saw it as in a dream—but two hours later he walked into Keswick. The total climb, twenty-five hours in duration, was fifty-three miles in length; the total footage scaled, 12,249 feet; and the fatigue equal to eighty-two miles level.

Mr. Jenkinson's walk created quite a stir, and ere long another champion arose in Leonard Pilkington, who had tramped from Liverpool to Windermere, a distance of eighty-four miles, in twenty-one hours, and also proved his quality on the fells. With Bennett, the Dungeon Ghyll guide, he passed over Bowfell, Scawfell Pike, Great Gable, Skiddaw, Saddleback, Helvellyn, and Fairfield in twenty-one hours thirty-four minutes, between 2 a.m. and 11 p.m. Mr. Pilkington says of this walk: 'We were both perfectly fresh at the finish, and had we come straight through, instead of having supper at Grasmere, we should have saved at least an hour—we could easily have done the journey in twenty hours ; but having finished the mountains, and with so much in hand, we did not think of it.' This tour necessitated climbing some 12,900 feet, and walking a distance of sixty miles, approximating in fatigue to eighty miles on the level.

October is not an ideal month for a scamper across the fells ; yet at this time of year Messrs. Robinson and Gibbs, the Lorton walkers, essayed to surmount the whole of the giants of Cumberland in twenty-four hours. On the stroke of midnight, Thursday, October 27, 1893, these gentlemen started from Keswick. A strong wind blew from the north-east, and the sky was too cloudy for more than mere gleams of moonlight as they walked up Borrowdale. By 2.10 a.m. Seathwaite was reached, the wakeful sheep-dogs making music as the climbers passed towards Great Gable. The dull roar of Taylor Ghyll Fall, and the rattle of the fierce wind on the higher levels, alone disturbed the hush of night. Snow-laden clouds swirled past them as they wound up the gully between the Gables, the air became bitter, a white mantle three inches thick covered the ground, and above a dense mist blotted out completely the summit. At 3.55 the top of the Grand Old Monarch was reached, and the Styehead Pass descended to. From the top a course was struck across the rough north-western face of the Scawfell Range, under Skew Ghyll, over a shoulder of Lingmell, and up to Lord's Rake, where in the closing days of 1893 Professor Milnes Marshall fell to his death.

In this cleft the scene was wild in the extreme. Snow lay thick, and outside its shelter the gale boomed and moaned among the great crags above. The scene was bleak and wintry ; the faces of the rock which were too abrupt for the snow to lie on were crusted with ice. From the top of the first reach of the Lord's Rake Messrs. Robinson and Gibbs struck off along the grassy ledge which gives easy access to Deep Ghyll. Here a sudden gust of wind loosened a stone high on the crags above, and they cowered under a rock as, with a crash and a bound through the air, it whizzed past into the dark recess immediately below.

The snow now became thicker, having been drifted into this wild ghyll by the wind, and on the steep bits near the top it was frozen sufficiently for them to kick their toes into the almost perpendicular slope, and go up it ladder fashion, holding on as best they could to insure safety. As the pair emerged on to the plateau on the top

of Scawfell at 6.10 a.m. the mists began to roll
away, and the first streaks of dawn were visible in
the east. Across the Mickledore, a fearful, rock-
split chasm, lay Scawfell Pike, to reach which
involved a descent to Broad Stand and a scramble
along the ice-coated ledges. Mr. Robinson says
of this portion of their experience : ' We were
not prepared to find the climb in a more dangerous
state than it was last year in midwinter, but such
it was ; and the alpenstocks we had provided ourselves with were without the usual spike in the
end with which to roughen the ice to make a
foothold. I took off the rucksack which held our
lunch, and, with an arm through one strap while
my friend held on to the other, kicked off the ice
from ledge to ledge.' Truly a risky mode of
progression, when a single slip would have had
irretrievable consequences.

The top of the Pikes was reached at 7.10 a.m.,
and thirty-five minutes later the couple were on
Great End. On the fells on every side the gale
was harrying the powdery snow. The tracks
over the passes were obliterated ; a landmark here
and there stood above the shifting plains of white.
Weird, dangerous, and black the crags stood over
their setting of whitened scree—a prospect which
cannot be described.

By this time the climbers must have been in a

comfortless state. Their clothes, damped by per-
spiration and half-molten particles of snow, would
long since be frozen to their backs. What that
means only those who have experienced it can
know. Bowfell, with one foot in Westmorland
and the other in Cumberland, was next in the
line, and here the ground, covered with shale and
masked with snow, became extremely dangerous.
The summit was found at 8.30 a.m., after which,
skirting the Langdale side of Hanging Knott,
Rossett Ghyll was descended to, and the tramp
over miles of bog to Wythburn begun. This
valley was reached by 12 a.m., and an hour and
twenty minutes later the ascent of mighty Helvellyn was commenced.

Thirlspot at 4 p.m. was the next point in the
tour. After passing through the Vale of St. John,
a halt was made for tea at Setmabanning, as the
moon was not yet up and it had begun to rain.
But at 6 p.m. the plucky climbers started for
Blencathra. The night became intensely dark,
the clouds denser, and the wind more and more
furious. Messrs. Robinson and Gibbs chose the
narrow ridge approach by Threlkeld to the mountain, as this afforded some shelter at first, but
on reaching the open the violence of the storm
was fearful ; only in the short lulls was progress
possible. Yet by 8.30 p.m. the summit was

reached, and the walkers plunged across the moors for Skiddaw.

After getting one-third of the way up this their last peak, they found that, though strength was still sufficient, time was not left to finish the ascent and reach Keswick ere another day. Accordingly, at 9.50 p.m. the finest pair of climbers the Lake District has ever seen turned back on the Glendaterra, reaching Keswick at 11.25 p.m. in extremely strong condition, considering the day's exertion.

Of the closing stage of the walk Mr. G. B. Gibbs says : ' It seems to me possible that we had quite sufficient time on leaving Threlkeld át 6 p.m.' to finish the attempt, ' but the darkness and very high wind, which caused us to take two and a half hours over the ascent of Blencathra, instead of one and a half hours (as we did four days later), made a loss of a very valuable hour. Further, the force of the wind as we rose from Skiddaw Forest was so great as to compel us to believe that progression would be on hands and knees when we got to the top, and produced a conviction that under these conditions we could not go the whole round within the day of twenty-four hours.'

Mr. Robinson is best described as a typical Cumberland man, endowed with a muscular system inherited from generations who revelled in outdoor life. As Dr. J. Norman Collie says: 'Robinson is the great authority on the hills of the Lake District. There is not a rock on a mountainside that he does not know. In sunshine or mist, in daytime or at midnight, he will guide one safely over passes or down precipitous mountainsides. Every tree and every stone is a landmark to him.'

The figures to represent this remarkable walk are: Distance, 56 miles in all—16 on the road and 40 on the fell—equalling in fatigue 86 miles of dead level. The total of height in feet reached was 13,840, the altitude of a considerable alp. The time was 23 hours 25 minutes, and the pace, taking the day's average, would be $4\frac{1}{2}$ miles per hour on the level, with more than $1\frac{7}{8}$ on the fell.

From 1893 to June of 1898 there was no serious attempt to claim the twenty-four hours' record, but during the month stated four Carlisle men—Messrs. Westmorland, Johnson, Strong, and Ernest Beaty—made a determined effort to put it to their credit. Their design was carried out under very favourable conditions. The men were in perfect training, had had a preliminary spin, and were rested for a start. This was from Seathwaite, right at the foot of the mountains—

not, as in previous records, from points more or less distant—on a clear morning, which merged into a bright and cool day. The party started at 5.27 a.m. in broad daylight, and immediately made for Great Gable, which was ascended in one hour eighteen minutes. The descent down the scree to Styehead Tarn was accomplished in eleven minutes, and a cast was made for Great End, reached in forty-three minutes.

This party took the Scawfell group by ascending its easier shoulder, not facing, as did Mr. Robinson, the dangerous scramble on the cliff-face by way of Skew Ghyll and Lord's Rake. Scawfell Pike was climbed at 8.4 a.m., and Mickledore crossed for Scawfell. The return by Broad Stand took thirty-six minutes—a different matter from Mr. Robinson's hazardous crossing — Eskhause being rereached at 9.31. Bowfell now loomed over Hanging Knott and Ewer Gap, and was ascended at 10.4, after which Wythburn was made for by way of Rossett Ghyllhead. At the Nagshead the party divided, two making for Threlkeld and home, the other pair for Helvellyn and beyond. The footgear of these two, it may be remarked — gymnasium slippers—was quite inadequate to the strains of fell-walking.

The remaining men now ascended Helvellyn, which took sixty-eight minutes, and walked along the descending tops to Threlkeld. Saddleback's ascent (from Threlkeld) occupied eighty - two minutes, and the walk across Skiddaw Forest to Skiddaw one and a half hours. What a different finish was this from the October night when Messrs. Robinson and Gibbs attempted to force their way through a howling tempest!

The moon now flooded the depression with peaceful light, but once across the summit the shadow of the hill was reached, and the path could only be followed with difficulty. Messrs. Johnson and Strong were fortunate enough not to get lost before they reached the valley, but here they made a mistake which cost them half an hour. On reaching the town of Keswick the walk was given up. It had extended over fifty-two miles of fell country; the total of altitude was 14,146 feet (294 feet more than Mr. Robinson's record); total time taken, nineteen hours thirty-five minutes. The average speed per hour was near two and a half miles; and in fatigue the course approached seventy-eight miles—eight miles less than the Lorton Walkers' record. The day was an ideal one—a day of bright sunshine, yet not overpowering heat. None of the party can ever forget the exquisite beauty of the scene at early morn as Seathwaite was left for Great Gable. The hills stood out in the deliciously pure air near to the eye, yet apparently dwarfed in height and retiring in perspective, but every crag, every cleft, every seam and line, in those majestic outlines was perfectly distinct. There is a difference in these two last-named walks which is hard to define; but the one resembled the other as much as a cycle race over sticky roads resembles the same event carried out on dry ground. Messrs. Johnson and Strong have shown themselves capable disciples of the older mountaineers, and their initial effort is sufficiently marvellous to puzzle criticism. In July, however, Mr. Westmorland and Mr. Beaty made another attempt to do the distance. They started from Threlkeld at 4.46 a.m. in bright sunshine, and took a line over Helvellyn, High Raise, Bowfell, Hanging Knott, Great End Crag, the Pikes, Scawfell, Great Gable, Skiddaw, and Saddleback, returning to Threlkeld.

The last part of this walk was accomplished in darkness, and the end was a close affair. After crossing the Caldew between Skiddaw and Saddleback at 2.40 a.m., this last mountain alone remained to be negotiated. Daylight was just beginning to show, but the higher ground was enshrouded in mist, and twenty valuable minutes were lost through the climbers missing their way. According to his own modest report, Mr. Westmorland began to lose heart here, fearing that the real top might not be found in the dense mist until the time was too far gone for success, but Mr. Beaty seemed as determined as ever. They could not decide as to which was the proper way up to the right summit of the mountain in the mist, so Mr. Beaty started off on the left-hand route, and Mr. Westmorland took that trending to the right. The latter proved to have chosen the right path, and shouted to Mr. Beaty, who joined him on the summit at 4.8 a.m. By this time only thirty-eight minutes remained of the set time, so, nerving themselves for a last almost desperate effort, the pair ran down the sharp edge of Saddleback—a rough, precipitous descent of over two miles and 2,800 feet, which was accomplished in twenty-two minutes. Such was the finish of a giant task. The course was completed in twenty-three and three-quarter hours—a magnificent performance. The nine fells had been climbed within twenty-four hours at the third attempt, and these two persevering men considered themselves rewarded.

It is granted that the month of September is the most favourable for walking, as the days are generally clear and cool ; therefore it not infrequently happens, as in 1898, that the season winds up with a record. At 3.30 a.m., September 1, Mr. R. W. Broadrick started on his cycle from Windermere for Dungeon Ghyll. When he started it was dark, so he left his machine in a conspicuous position, hoping that the hotel people would take charge of it. He climbed by way of Ell Ghyll to Bowfell, reaching the summit at 5.55 a.m. Day broke as he made the tour of the Scawfell group— Great End, Scawfell Pike, Scawfell. There is in Nature nothing on so grand a scale as a rosy day-break seen from some high mountain. The famous Wastdalian, Will Ritson, used to tell of what he witnessed from Scawfell Pikes. After following the hounds all night, he found himself by Mickle-dore when the light began to glow, and never having seen sunrise from such a position, he climbed the Pikes. He always referred to the sight as the finest he ever saw. Mr. Broadrick breakfasted at Wastdalehead, and then climbed by Gavel Neese to Great Gable, reaching Keswick by 12.50. On the way to Skiddaw the climber missed the path, and had to wade through knee-deep heather for about an hour. Keswick rereached, he made for Sticks Pass, by which route he gained Helvellyn by 7.40. Mr. Broad-rick went hard from here, hoping to get into Grasmere valley ere complete darkness fell. At Grisedale Tarn, however, the last gleams faded; he missed the way, and after stumbling across very rough ground (the south face of Seat Sandal) he reached the top of Dunmail Raise at 8.50. The walk to Windermere—thirteen miles—took two hours fifty-five minutes—a fine performance considering previous exertions. The total distance was sixty and a half miles, in the excellent time of twenty and a quarter hours. Mr. Broadrick's cycle played a very important part in the day's work, placing him while still fresh at the foot of the mountains; but deducting the twelve miles, and one hour thus passed, the performance remains a great one—forty-eight and a half miles for nineteen and a quarter hours. The total of height ascended is 13,450 feet, with a fatigue equivalent of sixty-six miles level, ignoring the twelve miles' cycle.

Excellent as were his previous walks, Mr. Broadrick has since done still better. He called on Mr. Westmorland, who has already been mentioned, and proposed that they should together try and beat all records by including Pillar Mountain and Fairfield in the walk, and doing the whole in twenty-four hours. Mr. Westmorland prepared a time-table, and they appointed to meet at Seathwaite. They journeyed, but the day proved wet and misty, and the walk was abandoned for that time. On September 14, 1901, in company with Mr. C. Dawson of Sale, Mr. Broadrick started from Rosthwaite at 3.32 a.m. The top of Styehead Pass was reached as day was breaking, the sharp ascent of Great Gable accom-

plished at 5.18. At this point Mr. Broadrick's
programme departed from the orthodox, for, instead
of descending again, he skirted Kirkfell and crossed
Black Sail Pass to the Pillar Mountain. The
ground here is very rough ; you are passing along
the ridge between two series of crag-climber's cliffs,
on which the Napes and the Pillar Stone need only
be mentioned. The quickest descent to Wastdalehead is down a long steep scree (the Doorhead),
and this was successfully done by 7.20 a.m. Here
the pair breakfasted, after which Mr. Oppenheimer
of Manchester joined them. The next group of
peaks assailed were those favourites of climbers—
Scawfell, Scawfell Pike, and Great End, where the
going is exceedingly rough. Between the first
and the second named mountains lies the Mickledore chasm—a great gap in the wall of rock—
whilst along the Pike and the following ridge is
a horrible *pave*, rocks many tons in weight lying
like so many tipped bricks, and over and among
these lies the route. The same class of surface is
also met with in Ewer Gap, save that there the
rocks are smaller. Mr. Broadrick's party reached
Scawfell at 8.45, the Pikes at 9.15, and Great
End at 9.41. Bowfell was passed at 10.25,
after which came the precipitous descent of the
Band to Dungeon Ghyll at 11.18. Mr. Evans
and a brother of Mr. Oppenheimer took the

party of record-makers on from this point, and
Grasmere was reached at 1.25. The next mountain
was Fairfield—a splendid scree-strewn giant—and
the party climbed this by 2.26. The quickest
descent from the summit is down a long series
of screes, quick work requiring surefootedness and
careful attention. The walk to Helvellyn top,
with a refreshing dip by the way in Grisedale Tarn,
was negotiated in an hour and a half. Thirlspot
was reached, and another excellent meal disposed
of, at 4.50. The evening now began to draw on,
and Saddleback's huge summit was made at 7.55.

' We went on very well till the top of Saddleback,' writes Mr. Broadrick, ' the weather conditions being perfect; but there darkness and fog
came down together, and we had five hours
stumbling along by compass and lantern-light,
which, owing to the mist, only showed up two or
three feet of the ground ahead at one time. Added
to that, there was a very strong north-east wind,
which blew the light out continually, and necessitated wrapping it up in a sweater. However,
after making up our minds several times that it
would be necessary to spend the night on the
uplands, we struck the railing leading down the
mountain. I don't know whether we got to
the actual top of triple-headed Skiddaw, but
we got to one of the tops, and stuck our cards

on the caërn. It was utterly impossible to tell which of the three it was.' Eventually, at 12.50, after much uncomfortable scrambling and many stumbles, they reached Keswick, and, tired but triumphant, Rosthwaite at 3.4 a.m., thus claiming the record, with half an hour to spare.

The length of this record walk must be over sixty-seven miles, involving ascents equivalent to 16,600 feet, and a fatigue equal to some ninety-two miles on the flat.

To speak about the men who have carried out these big walks is difficult, but the greatest moderns are a splendid contrast. Mr. Westmorland is a splendidly developed man of over fifty years of age—Sandow's gold medalist for his county; whilst Mr. Broadrick is a tall, lithe young man full of wire and go—the ideal of a climber and wrestler with the elements, in my opinion. Mr. Broadrick can perhaps average half a mile per hour better than his rival in a straight walk; but Mr. Westmorland's splendid stamina and perseverance, together with his lifelong study of methods of climbing and descending, give him a strong pull when the two are compared. As an aside with a tremendous bearing on the subject, both are well-known crag-climbers : Mr. Broadrick, with his brothers, just failed to surmount the last overhanging cornice of Walker's Gully in the

famous Pillar Rock a few weeks before the late
O. G. Jones and the brothers Abraham carried the
whole ascent.

As I am passing these pages for press (June),
news has come to hand that even Mr. Broadrick's
record has been beaten. Mr. S. B. Johnston, of
Carlisle, at 5 a.m. on May 28, started from Threlkeld for the Sticks Pass and Helvellyn. This
summit was gained at 7.20, Fairfield at 8.19, and
the descent to Grasmere negociated by 9.12.
After passing Grasmere, Mr. Johnston and his
pacer, Mr. Strong, pushed over Red Bank to
Langdale, where at Stool End (10.55) Mr. Westmorland was waiting. He conducted over Bowfell (12.0), and right down the Scawfell range.
Here the ground is extremely rough. The day
was excessively hot ; yet good progress was made.
Wastdalehead was reached at 3.20, and the long
Doorhead Pass to Pillar Mountains essayed. A
journey in the hollow of the fells here made genial
James Payn assert that the Lake Country—and
Wastdale in particular—was the hottest part of
England. The ground from the Pillar (4.33) to
Great Gable is very difficult to cross with speed ;
yet Mr. Johnston's twelve hours of exertion had
told but little here. Seathwaite was descended to
7.25 p.m., a really good piece of walking. Mr.
Johnston allowed forty-five minutes here for rest

and refreshment, after which, with Mr. Beaty in
front, he did the nine miles to Keswick (two of
them moderate mountain road) under the two
hours. Nor did the gathering darkness in any
way diminish the pace up Spooney Green Lane
on the way to Skiddaw. At exactly midnight this
summit was reached, and careful direction for Blencathra, last summit of the circle, taken. The two
walkers marked out a course by the stars, and so
kept their proper line. At 2.10 a.m. the summit
of Blencathra was reached. The descent which
remained is a very steep one. The ridge leading
down to the lead-mines needs the greatest care at
all times, and at that early hour it was not light
enough to distinguish grass from rock. Also a
strong breeze was blowing, which made balance
on the narrow ridge a difficult matter. Fifty
minutes were taken for the descent—in July, 1898,
Mr. Westmorland and Mr. Beaty did it in twenty-
two minutes at a later period of morning—and
Trelkeld, the starting-point, was reached at 3.7 a.m.
The whole journey therefore took twenty-two
hours seven minutes—a remarkable performance.

I am averse to summing up and comparing
the figures quoted in this chapter, but one
advantage the later record-makers have assumed :
pacing and prearrangement of all kinds is considered necessary, and the record-maker is relieved

of all impedimenta. Similarly, many of the mountain tracks have been much improved by use and judicious repair during the period under review, so that the number of cases in which it is an advantage to a strong walker to leave the orthodox route are now few indeed.

In conclusion I desire to acknowledge my indebtedness for many kindnesses and much valuable information to the walkers whose journeyings it is my pleasure to chronicle.

The last has not been heard of the 'fell-walking' records, and I trust athletes will ever be forthcoming with hearts as plucky and limbs as stout as those of the men I have written of.

THE COMPLETE RAMBLER

THE COMPLETE RAMBLER

I. Up the Dale

BENEATH the trees in the orchards the early snow-drops are the only wild-flowers; hollies and other evergreens stand out sombre and heavy amid the sere woodlands; the closest observation reveals not an opening bud on the hardiest hedge-row. Everything is gray and dead and cold between the bridge over the rock chasm and the distant fells, where in the ghylls and hollows small fields of snow contrast chill white to the dim blue slopes around.

Such is my argument, and yet——

To begin with, the bridge beneath our feet is interesting; a score varieties of hardy ferns thrive in its crevices. The beck rushes twenty feet below its single arch, churning round in a basin scooped by its own rude efforts here, rushing with feeble thunder over an abrupt rock there, sliding in green volumes down a smooth slab anon, to settle finally in a narrow rock-bound pool. Wrens are already flitting about the dense masses of ivy which trail over one side of the gorge—opposite the gray outer wall of the old mill—the longest fairy-rope hanging nearly halfway to the pellucid waters. And what is this skimming in jerky flight upstream —a little bird decked in blue and red splendours? Where the mill-wheel resounds to the thumping of hidden waters, and lazily draws round its dripping, mossy buckets, the kingfisher hangs a second in the air. Were you to descend, you would find a ' rat-hole ' there, in a seam of clay between heavy strata of rock, the mouth partially veiled by the rushing spent-water from the wheel. A few years have passed since, with the heedlessness of youngsterdom, I scrambled from this bridge down to the water-wheel. The mill was not working at that hour, but a fair current of water poured down the spent-way. I was standing ankle-deep in this, gazing up at the great wheel, when there was a faint snatch of a kingfisher's song outside, and I turned to watch its burnish of blue and red glint past in the sunshine. But the bird turned, and, without abating its speed, dashed into the veil of descending water close to my feet. A minute later I had turned this aside, and was possessed of the kingfisher's secret. Two neat bluish eggs reposed within the crevice on a bed of fish-bones, etc. Year after year the bird had hatched her brood in the sound of the mill-wheel without discovery. That bird pausing in its flight knows of the hidden dwelling, perchance has called it 'home,' and is now thinking of paying it an early visit. But no! as it wavers it notes strange appearances above the bridge. It flirts forward, beneath us, a line of flashing metallic sheens, and goes winging upstream at a tremendous pace.

From the bridge, northward, past the stone mounting-block. Close beside, in white gushing founts, the beck is fretting its way down a rugged channel. Here and there a rock is crowned with a gray patch of grass. In summer this will be an islet of glory, its rich green pall beneath a cloud of dancing blue harebells and golden-eyed white ghoods (marguerites). The hillsides towering around are gray—gray streaked with broad lines and patches of green bog-moss and water-grass ; along their slopes great boulders are strewed. These vagrant rocks are most plentiful near the cliff. Our eye catches a faint dot hovering above : a buzzard hawk—since the raven retired to less accessible peaks—the monarch of these wilds. A colony of rooks inhabit a cluster of oak-trees beside the road, their hoarse caws rising over the tumult of surging waters. Just here the river takes a sharp turn, and we are suddenly brought in sight of an old and disused bobbin-mill. Time was—and deserted Cocks Close mill is a memento of it—when the trade of bobbin-making was prosperous in this and many another contiguous valley. Three mills—one near the bridge, this at Cocks Close, and one further upstream, which has completely disappeared as a building, though its excavated waterways remain—were in full swing, and every cottage for miles around was inhabited. Cocks Close is beyond the stream. A couple of thick spruces have been laid side by side, and span the chasm. Walk upon them. They sway fearsomely. Do not touch that hand-rail: of its four posts, not one is soundly fixed, and some day soon the forty feet of rail will fall away of its own accord. The two trees sag differently under our weight, so that on the perilous passage your right foot is often placed on a quivering log a foot lower than that supporting your left. I crossed here once on a wild November evening; a gale was blowing, and the river was in full flood. In the scant light prevailing great darkling jets seemed to toss within a foot of the trembling structure. Daring beyond discretion, I waited for a lull in the storm, and then started to cross. I had not got more than halfway, when, with a sharp, snarling roar, the furies were around me. It probably happened in a second, but the time seemed long hours to me. The powerful gale gradually pressed me further and further over; the frail black pathway over those dancing waters seemed to fail, and I felt something must soon give way. After a long interval my mind began to work. I threw myself flat on the pine bridge, holding on with hands and feet till the wild gust spent itself. I don't care to be in such a position again.

Further up the dale the river goes far away from the road; we see it across the fields occasionally. Yonder is a heron fishing, or, more likely, feasting on fish which have met with death on the spawning-redds. Friend Jammie is a well-known beckside bird here, and we will possibly meet him later at closer quarters. That cock crows in a peculiar high-pitched clarion. Yet that is the call of the real fighting cock. The bird is leisurely strolling across the road with its harem, or 'mantling aboot as if t' farm belonged to it,' as its owner avers. Stop a moment, and I will ask him about the bird and cock-fighting.

'Ay, Tam's varra fair,' shortly admits the dalesman, in reply to my spoken admiration of his champion. As he speaks he eyes me curiously. This sort of conversation from a stranger means either that the other is of the 'cocker' cult or an ally of the powers that be ranged against that interesting sport.

'My, but his spurs are short!' I remark as innocently as I can possibly muster.

A glimmer of recognition lights up his face.

'It's thee, is it? I didn't ken thee. What, man! I've nivver seen thee sen that main as was brokken up by t' police.'

The dalesman apparently recollects myself and that occasion well, for did he not mount guard over me? Wandering over a lonely moor, up hill and down dale, I suddenly walked into a cock-pit. Two men had just released their birds, which were prancing around the tiny greensward, hectoring one another and gradually infuriating themselves to an attack. I had wandered through the line of scouts, always, in these days of persecution, posted by watchful 'cockers'; but being where I was and a mere stripling, I was compelled to stay, lest I should put the authorities on the track, and, indeed, had got somewhat interested in the sport, when a sudden alarm caused the ring to disperse hurriedly. As I sped away, I saw the enraged cocks still battling wildly on the arena, and saw two or three sacks, which evidently contained other feathered gladiators, lying on the ground some yards away. Celerity in putting myself through the cordon of police alone saved me from being haled before the magistrates with the 'cockers' and their birds.

'Dosta ken Tam? he is the varra [very] spit an' image o' t' bird as wod ha' [would have] won t' main on t' fell.'

Yes, now I remember. What a beautiful form that bird had! Tam is as like it as two peas. Not leggy and tall, but compact in build, a fighter of a fighting strain. Glorious red plumage as close in texture as leather, stout thighs beneath whose short feathers the muscles quiver. But who can describe the fighting cock? There is a distinction about its movements, a pride in the poise of its head, the contour of which, though wattles and comb are clipped short, is still beautiful. But beauty and majesty are to be expected in an inheritor of three centuries of bluest blood; and as for courage, neither weight nor size matters much to the fighting cock. Like the other pet of the dalesmen, the trail-hound, it is trained to go to a finish, odds be as they may. A fighting cock and a turkey-cock were holding an impromptu main the other day in a farmyard until actively interfered with. A few words more of admiration of his pet puts the dalesman entirely at his ease, and he breaks freely into reminiscences and explanation.

'How do we fit the spurs on to a fighting-cock? Well, wait a minute and I'll show you.' He steps into the whitewashed cottage, and in a few seconds returns with a pair of polished steels. 'These are the spurs; they're of the varra [very] best steel, and you mun [must] mind, because they're sharp. My father hes a pair of silver ones that his grandfather wan [won] when a lad of sixteen, at a girt [great] main at Ooston [Ulverston] Fair. There used to be some cocking then, but, of course, noo it's called illegal.' Now flamed forth the ire of a republican country-side. 'And why was it forbidden? For nowt [nothing] else than because the quality couldn't show off and win all t' mains. Old Squire ——, grandfather of him that hes the Bank Hall now, paid many a hundred pound trying to pit a bird that could stand up to the first four in t' dale when Lady Mary's bell* was fought for.'

'How do you fix these spurs?'

'Well, you see'—the verbal storm had passed, and the cocker was in earnest on his sport—'the cock's spurs are shaved down as far as possible, then'—Tam, seeing the gleaming weapons and scenting a battle, had strolled up to us, so with a dexterous sweep of the arm the dalesman captured him and gave us an object-lesson on the craft—'these are slipped on—they just fit—over the spur, and fastened round the leg. Now'—releasing

---

* The prize at the chief mains in the old time was a small silver bell, which was worn by the victorious bird, or by its master when his champion was actively engaged.

Tam, who forthwith set up a defiant and hasty crowing—' he's fit to fight, except that his comb and wattles would have to be shorn.'

' In cock-fighting the most active and alert bird wins. The birds face each other and try to jump, so that when descending the sharp spurs will cut into their opponent which is, of course, beneath. The wounds in cock-fighting, save for occasional pecks, are almost always on the head, neck, and back. Most are slight, the thick felting of feathers stopping all but the most directly delivered strokes. Some cockers, when the birds are fairly set to, will not allow them to be separated, but I never let my cock down into a ring unless it is agreed that any fighter cut down—that is, knocked off its feet with a blow from the spurs—is considered beaten. Most cockers want to see a kill, and they have their way.'

' Not much cocking done nowadays, you think. Well, as it's you, and ye've seen a bit of it, I wod [would] say that there's more going on now than ivver there's been sen cock-fighting was put down. I know a dozen gentlemen, men with big estates and fine houses, as are magistrates and on t' County Council, as hod [hold] many a main, and they say one parson isn't again tekkin' [taking] a bird on if it's kept quiet. Way over Furness, there's hundreds and hundreds of cockers, man, and more every year, and it's a bonny sport more to them as takes an interest in it.'

So saying, the dalesman turns to again admire his pet. A stranger is coming along the road— our friend swoops down on the bespurred Tam and bears him out of sight ; we, feeling somewhat guilty, walk on up the dale.

The river is again close by ; a slight bank separates it from the road. The waters are babbling pleasantly over a long array of shingles ; here and there an attenuated trout fins languidly along. The spawning season has just passed ; these valley becks are shallow, with no deep, silent pools to hold an almost inexhaustible supply of fish-food. So shallow is even the main stream on the redds that, when a long frost causes it to dwindle in volume, the fish are often frozen down to the gravel their eggs are deposited in. When the thaw floods come, the dead bodies are washed far away, into odd corners beneath bending willows and behind rocks, food in plenty for otter and heron.

Here is a bridge of the old type, tall of arch and narrow of roadway, and crowning the short ascent in front is the churchyard. It boasts a sundial, but it is loose on a decaying post. The church itself is quite a new one, superseding a mouldy, dark building of unknown antiquity. Yet the building is interesting, for does it not contain the archives of the dale—wondrously complex churchwarden accounts dating back over a hundred years, and rich in personal touches of old-time men and women? The churchwardenship was then the most responsible position in the valley; the holder was directly responsible for the welfare of the poor. Charity was dispensed with sound judgment, and only to relieve necessity. The famous Smit Book is here, but, alas! it is no longer carried by the priest* to the nearest Shepherds' Meet in order that disputes may be properly settled, and lost sheep, by their fleece and horn-marks, traced.

The valley is now opening out; to right and left great rock-strewn bluffs bound its almost level bed. Floods are of frequent occurrence here, but they run off the land quickly. I have waked at dawn. Since midnight a storm had raged, and great films of falling rain crashed resoundingly against window and door of our cottage. Outside the level of the dale is occupied by a sullen lake, stretching far toward the mountains; the rain-squalls are ploughing its surface with wide white furrows. The storm ceases suddenly; the cloud-banks trail reluctantly from the fells, revealing a

* Among the fells the Church of England minister has been from time immemorial named 'the priest.'

paradise of falling waters. Six hours later the broad acres are showing green and soaked, and the river is back in its channel. Such brief life, though furious, has a flood of the fell lands.

Through the leafless alders lining the ghylls we see, in gushing white, rivulets descending from the unseen moors. On our right Gray Crag heaves up its plainer, grassier shoulder; and next to it is Anchorite's Breast, where in a shallow cave by the beckside legend says an anchorite from the monastery at Shap dwelt many a year. The monks in this district seem to have been very self-contained in their dealings, and were much misunderstood by the half-pagan, half-Christian Saxons about them. It is stated that the dwellers in the dale refused to furnish the hermit with food. His weary track over the long moor to the abbey can, it is averred, even now be traced.

But to-day, instead of pensive monks, on the wild gray tracts of grass are seen men moving at a run. The dalesman loves a fox-hunt dearly. He is tireless in the pursuit. Miles of open country glide beneath his feet. On the rough crags and moraines his dexterity is marvellous. The hunt is in full cry on the hillside. The hounds are going at a great pace; the men are every moment further and further in the rear. A

quick eye might even catch the tiny brown form of
the fox running for its very life. For some minutes
we watch them sweep along, at first parallel to the
dale, then gradually turning up and up the mountainside to its crest. Hound after hound leaps
on to the tall wall, halts a brief second, his form
outlined against the bright blue sky, then dis-
appears, and faint, long-drawn-out voices are all
we have of a mountain fox-hunt.

As we turn away we begin to meet numbers of
the chase. They tell us the pack are well up to
their fox, that they will hunt him in the next dale,
maybe, but unless they kill they will bring him
back again. Maybe about Yewbarrow, says one,
as he trudges briskly along ; about Swinbank,
argues another, and takes things more leisurely.
Now two men in pink are coming towards us.
What a change to eyes full of sombre gray and
green is a flash of warm colour ! It is the veteran
master of the pack and his huntsmen. The dalesmen salute the elder cheerfully. He has a word
for all, and a pleasant one, too. He is wiry in
build ; his genial face is wrinkled. He has doffed
black hunting-cap ; his hair, cropped short beneath,
is silvern. This is the man who for two generations has provided sport in the dales. John Peel
was not less deserving of the grand hunting-song
than he is. With a courteous salutation he passes

us by. Many a time I have thought of and sighed for the splendid hunts he has witnessed both before and since the last 'greyhound' fox was killed.

A mile further on the road crosses a short rise caused by an outcropping vein of white felspar. To the right is one of those conical mounds dubbed by dalesmen either 'ancient fortresses,' 'barrows,' or 'haycocks,' formed by the glacial process of denudation and deposit in days long past.

For a couple of hours it has seemed as though we were walking along a level, but from this slight eminence we see that the dale is but as a shelf sloping downwards from the mountains. The bluffs which dominated the view at our starting are now insignificant in the distance, and we look over their tops to a broad, undulating valley. In front of us is the dalehead, a small subvalley, the entrance a narrow 'gate' between two converging ribs of mountain, the exit a rugged track winding up rock-strewn braes.

There is but one tenement in sight, an ancient sheep-farm perched quite close to the rocky river-bed. Its buildings are very old ; one or two possess floors of trodden earth probably dating back four hundred years. The yeoman who possesses the domain is much respected. Further up the stream than Sacgill is a level strewn with beaches of stone. Here at some time has been a small lake, but the torrents have completely buried it in débris. Their activity is so great that the whole dale has to contribute to the cost of a retaining barrier here. Otherwise in a single winter 10,000 tons of stones would be washed down, the river-bed would be choked for miles, and the stream would run riot down the dale, turning into marshy bogs what are now carefully-drained pastures. The prophecy of 'Every valley shall be exalted, and every hill brought low,' was once preached from a dales pulpit. 'But net in oor day [but not in our time], O Lord!' fervently ejaculated an aged hearer.

The dalehead, as we travel into it, presents rather a dreary aspect. Even the bogs are gray, not green as on lower heights. A few thin patches of scrubby coppice show on the slopes immediately behind the farm ; a little patch of soil near the opening of a deep ghyll is clothed with a large plantation. Gray grass and tangles of rotting bracken are on the braes, but the area of naked rock, scree, and scattered boulders far exceeds these. The whole outlook is barren and forbidding. How can a farmer wrest a living from such a place? How indeed! The sheep-farm is barely remunerative in these days of cheap wool ;

but mountain mutton is renowned, though the producer benefits little by this.

In about half an hour we reach the choked tarn area. When its dark waters laved the lowermost scree-beds of these steep fells, the dalehead must have made a perfect picture. Even now to our left Goat Scaur raises its grand head nearly 2,000 feet above us, while on our opposite side in one huge cliff the Gray Crag stands almost as high. Both mountains are plenteously splashed with white. On the lower pitches the snow in the deepest gullies are remains of great drifts, but as the eye rises higher the white areas become more numerous ; they are connected one with another, and at the top of the brae a long white curling drift resists the spring sunlight. The level beams of eventide shoot over the hills from westward, flushing the snowfields with crimson bars and glorious rosy shadows. At last, by a rough, water-torn road, we reached the summit of the pass, 2,000 feet or so above sea-level,

'With a tumultuous waste of huge hilltops before us,'

Kidsty Pike, where the wild deer of Martindale often roam. On a day like this we saw over the glistering snow-fields a stag and three hinds galloping toward Swindale, a splendid sight ! Branstree, a rounded mammoth on our left, is the home of giant foxes ; many a stiff run has

started from its benks (grass ledges). The deeper
hush of night is even now falling on the voiceless
wastes. Hark! what is that? The crunching of
a foot in the snow, and round a corner in the pass,
toiling upwards, comes a dalesman. We hail him
with delight, for the very air breeds lonesomeness.

' I was just coming from Mardale,' says he. 'I've
been driving a few sheep over as had strayed.'

He is a man of rather more than middle age,
hard, wiry, full of vigour and life.

' How long have you lived in this valley?' I
ask.

' Was born here at a little house halfway down
the dale; you'll remember it—there are a few
sap-trees overhanging it. Just before you came to
that farm where dead foxes are hanging in t' trees.'

' Been a shepherd all your life?'

' Well, yes; I was ten year old when I began
to shepherd on t' fell hard aside of home. Things
were a bit different then.'

The sound of a triple tramp on the snow-
patched road is all that is heard for a few moments;
then, from its feast of carrion beside a rock, a
great raven soars croaking up, up, up, high above
the dale to where the sun still reigned. The sight
of this swooping bird fills the shepherd with wrath.

' Ay, thoo may croak,' he says sadly, ' but
maybe we'll be the better of thee in nesting-time.'

Then to us : 'Those ravens are a nuisance. Every spring we have to go out nesting to keep down their numbers. They think little of attacking a weakly lamb and carrying it off among the rocks.

'I remember well one day we went after some ravens in Goat Scaur front. Four shepherds joined me and we took plenty of ropes. Getting opposite where I thought the nest was, we descended the cliff as far as there was foothold. On the last ledge a gavelock [crowbar] was fixed to let out the rope by ; then, tying a noose round my body, I stepped and downward. I could hear the old bird croaking away beneath. My mates kept letting the rope come slowly, and, of course, I went down with equal speed. At last, when I should think some fifty feet of rope had been let out, I stopped on a narrow ledge.

'Looking cautiously about, I soon found traces of my quest : on that jutting rock it seemed that father raven had sat watching his mate sitting her couple of eggs. I carefully clambered forward to the splinter, and to my joy found the raven's nest in sight. But in a moment my hopes were dashed. A deep narrow crack lay between me and my goal. Try as I would, the gulf could not be passed, and the old raven sitting there in security seemed to croak derision at me. However, by returning to my companions and being relowered from some more favourable spot, I hoped yet to turn the tables. So up I went, assisting my friends by rapid runs up any face of rock which gave a possible angle. In a moment I explained the situation and we were traversing the great cliff in the desired direction. When a platform for our rope-head was found, I made another descent; but, instead of the straight course I had fancied possible, a great rock overhanging the gully sent me dangling in mid-air, unable to reach foothold. However, it was possible to avoid the ugly cornice and then I climbed down the side of the gully. The old raven flapped off her nest with a wild croak as I came near, but she never went far away. More than once, with a whistling swoop, she came almost within arms' length, and every time I prepared to parry some sudden attack with beak or wings. Probably, had her mate been within call they would not have hesitated to attack me, for in defence of its nest the raven is pretty vicious. As soon as they were within reach, I scooped up the eggs from the barrowful of filth— remains of rats and carrion lay on a bed of wool and sticks—and was rapidly drawn up to safety. One raven was shot shortly afterwards, at which the other left the neighbourhood. A good riddance for us shepherds, too!'

II. Harvest-time on the Fells

As I wandered in solitary thought across the moor I heard voices in front of me. As the tones were in complete accord with my mood and with that region of cheerful silence, I was but mildly curious as to their origin. I lingered on the summit of a splintered outcrop of rock and looked around me. To my eye the scene was perfect. The heather was in full bloom; the air was resonant with the humming of bees, intent on petty plundering of the purple flowerets; around the heather-beds were here and there solid banklets of dainty crimson and white heatherbell, and next them the harebell's large sky-blue corolla curtseying on its slender stalk to every swerve of the breeze. Beneath the domain of the hardy heather a waving green wilderness marked the haunt of the bracken, very rugged with fragments in its upper portion, from the crumbling hillside above, but lower down opening out an almost level ledge of the mountain.

Descending leisurely to this, I recognised some of my neighbours at work among the bracken. One was cutting the stout stems with a scythe, leaving a thick swath behind him, which another spread out so that the sun's rays might dry it. Some two score yards away three other men were loading a sleigh with the dark-brown harvest cut some days ago, and now ready for the barn. This was a great contrast to the lowland hayfield of the farm. The ground, which from above looked so smooth and almost level, was in reality furrowed with innumerable watercourses and seamed with rocky places. One moment the sleigh timbers creaked as a sudden strain was put upon them by an unseen hollow; next the stout, handy horse drew it clear of this, and the runners were sliding with unpleasant grinding sound over a pavement of boulders. These men had been on the moors since soon after daybreak, and shortly they would have to return to their farms. I assisted to bind on the dusky load, and made down the hillside in their company. The path taken by the rude conveyance was, it seemed to me at first, a dried-up watercourse; it fell so steeply that at places our combined resistance alone prevented the sleigh from overrunning the sturdy little mare in front, while the unevenness kept us continually on the alert lest the load should, as the dalesmen put it, 'keck ower' at some particularly awkward point. But the cautious and sure-footed animal in the traces brought down the load with safety to the level of the mountain tarn, of which we had enjoyed almost a bird's-eye view.

In our Lake Country dales it is impossible to grow enough straw for bedding purposes in winter, and the hayfield is often insufficient for forage ; therefore the farmer turns to the uplands and draws thence the necessary supplies. Large areas of bracken are cut every year, and by primitive sleigh routes brought down to where carts can be used conveniently. The scythe used in cutting bracken is a much shorter contrivance than the ordinary one, but the work is more tiring. The ground is so covered with stones or otherwise uneven that but seldom can the labourer get two swinging strokes together, and the perpetual jerking to avoid the blade being damaged accounts for many a man's dislike to the work.

A couple of gamekeepers as we came to the mereside were preparing a boat to row to the other end of the tarn, and, as I wished to ramble in that direction, I embarked with them. In the clear, peaty depths trout were lazily finning in and out among the gently-swaying water-weeds, and smaller fry disported nearer the surface. As we approached one point the keepers ceased rowing, in order that we might float over where a large pike lay in wait for its prey, and at a rocky islet ran ashore that I might inspect the trees where the recently shot vermin were gibbeted. The boat was forced through a fringe of blue irises to the mouth of a tiny beck, where I landed. Soon the faintly-rutted track I was following changed direction, and I struck across the heathy waste. Grouse rushed away with querulous cries, curlew and heron banished silence from the wilds, while from tussock and cevin small birds chirped and twittered. A lark high above was singing a joyous roundelay; suddenly his ringing notes were hushed, and down from his crazy height he rushed, for the raucous voice of a buzzard struck terror to the tiny winger. Wave after wave of moorland—a sameness which might almost become monotony. Each hollow, opening out its treasures, gave the same tiny stream, with myriad sphagnum bogs and stunted willows; every shallow glen was carpeted with bracken and heather. But now a change.

A great knot of fir-trees rose on the near horizon; and as I stepped up the stony ridge to which they anchored with huge cablelike roots, in front there appeared a series of distant blue mountains—the heights of Lakeland—while nearer at hand stretched outward a long triangular plateau, its apex touching the nearest fell, its base the ridge on which I stood. In about the middle of this expanse was a fairly large tarn. In about half an hour I was close to its shores. As the lower ground was reached, a score small tumuli met my eye, and on approach these proved to be of peat—miniature stacks loosely piled, so that the air circulated freely through them, and though built wet, their contents would soon become dry. At the tarn edge I spent some minutes in collecting the fine yellow water-lilies, which occur only in this tarn in our vicinity; then, espying a man at work in the distance, I made in his direction. The intervening space was swampy; sometimes by a series of grass banks I gained far, only to be stopped by a spongy bog too wide to leap. But here and there, retracing my steps, I gradually found a track across the maze; the man was mowing the reeds which in wide stretches favour such surroundings—not an easy task when the disproportion of sound land is considered. Of course, he only mowed the more accessible places; but even then he had to garner the cut stems on a hand sleigh, and draw them to a hillside where the tarn waters, if overpent after a thunder-storm, were little likely to reach. The reeds also were to be used for winter bedding; and so large a quantity is required in the dales abutting the plateau that half a dozen barns for their summer storage are in the immediate vicinity of the swamps.

Half a mile on—I was now facing eastward to reach one of the valleys—I came across a party of men digging peat. The heather tufts had been burnt away, and the thin veil of soil thrown aside to lay bare the deposits. Then, with a long narrow spade, cuts were made in the chocolate-coloured pile, so that an oblong mass was easily separated, and these were collected and wheeled aside to be piled into the loose erections previously mentioned. The dexterity of the spademan was pretty to watch; the blade of the tool was plied as freely and easily as a knife. Peat-digging on the flanks of the fells is easy compared with the same work on the lowlands, for here drainage is rapid and sufficient, and the deposits less dense and moist. Many of the dales farms still use little other fuel but peat and coppice-wood. As I stood near the labourers, I noticed a violet in bloom—a rare occurrence on such an exposed situation—and into my mind rushed an anecdote of Wonderful Walker, Vicar of the mountain parish of Sea-thwaite a century ago, whose life of industry and nobility of character claimed the admiration of William Wordsworth. Said he : 'See you that violet?'—pointing to a little simple pansy that was bending its graceful flower close to the spot on which he stood. 'Look at it, and think how it came there. Last autumn this spot was covered with bog-earth, which had probably rested on this bleak and barren moor ever since the Deluge. It was disturbed last year by the spade of the turf-getter, and now this beautiful flower has sprung up in this place! For ages and ages its seed must have remained embedded in this sour and barren bog; yet, once disturbed by the hand of man, it springs up fresh and lively, to show that God can keep alive what to the eye of man may seem to perish, and can deck with grace and beauty even the most unpromising spots of creation.'

III. A Mountain Ramble

DIVERSE are days among the fells—some wet,
some fine. On some the mountains seem to pal-
pitate in sultry haze; on others they stand statue-
like and distinct against the bright blue skies of
spring and autumn. The rocks and slopes possess
ever-changing moods: grim with snow and icicles
in early spring, green with grass and fern and moss
later on, russet and crimson with the dying fires of the
fall, gray and wan washed with the rains of winter.

*　　*　　*　　*　　*

Eskdale in the pride of summer. The woods
are covered with heavy foliage; in the bright
morn light the brackens clothing the rocky tors
waves, and their fronds sparkle with drops of
glory. Down the glens and over the rocks bright
rivulets are dashing; sunny waters are sleeping in
every hollow. The air feels buoyant, leaping with
life, as though all Nature were revelling after the
dun span of night. Thus for half an hour, till a
cloud-bank swirls up from seaward. A dark

shadow stalks along the valley; great billows of rain slash against the trees and rattle among the quivering leaves. The mountains, fringed and studded with rock, seem to throw back the storm-wrack from their sides; they tower dimly through the dark tide of drops, and as each brief paroxysm subsides they peer down again on the soaked dale. Then the squall passes on as rapidly as it came: the cap of wind soughs itself out among the swaying branches, and in a minute the air is clear, the sky blue and joyous, and with a flash the sun looks through the fast-retiring beards of mist and rain, cheering the dripping woods and bedrenched meadows, rousing skylark from the field, thrush in the brake, gilding the hurrying, foaming rills and beds of watery fern. So, with regular portions of rain and fair weather, passed two hours of the morning.

When I started the air was clear; a gray bank of cloud was wandering among the distant mountains. The bright sun glinted on Eskdale's emerald braes and laughing cataracts. A cloudlet of steam marked the laborious approach of the tiny decrepit train which runs between Boot and Ravenglass. Many years ago a geologist traced a rich outcrop of hematite in the hills here. Capital was easily found to exploit the series of mines; labourers in hundreds flocked to the old-world valley. Nine miles of light railway were hurriedly laid. Then the mines suddenly 'petered' out. The expected El Dorado was a mere surface-seam of ore. Now ghylls and hillsides hide the great abrasions of that brief dawn of human energy 'neath deep bracken and heath. The costly machinery at the pits is mere scrap, not worth transport; at some places the whole outer structure has fallen down great declivities, to rust in tangled, dismal ruin. The cabins of the miners have almost entirely disappeared; the cottages, unroofed and with trembling walls, are nearly gone. On my right the river was running with surcharged speed. Its banks could not hold its volume; the alders and rowans rooted in the water's realm shook as the current buffeted them. Every hundred yards or so an islet divided the force of the stream. Channels long ago deserted by the river were full and strong again, surrounding large slices of meadowland, on which kingcups bloomed in profusion.

After about half an hour's walk, I turned in where a bridge spans a gorge, where Esk would be tumbling and churning and roaring in flood lust and fury. Yesterday hardly a foot of water flowed quietly far beneath the bridge, but now the raving torrent, pent in by immovable rocks, shot beneath the arch, throwing up, as obstacles buried

far beneath were struck, a smother of spray. The
water had risen eight feet during the night at this
point, and was probably still rising. From a rock
ledge next the bridge a veteran angler was trying
for sea-trout. Again and again he swung his line
into the wild turmoil of currents. Possibly this
man had been out since daybreak, for the sea-fish
were running in large numbers. While I was
present two fine fish came to his net. The second,
aided by the tremendous power of the down-
coming waters, made a splendid and exciting fight.
Esk in flood is never more than mildly turgid,
and it was not difficult to follow the fish's evolu-
tions. Once, with a vicious backward leap, I
thought it had broken clear; but my veteran had
anticipated such a move, and his line ran slack
accordingly.

'Catch many?' I asked.

'Season's been rayther bad till noo,' was his
reply. 'It's oor first spate, this, and near t' end
of August, too.'

'How have you done this morning?'

'Varra fair. Twelve, but they're nobbut lile
uns' [only little ones]. Which to my mind
was a fiction. That second sea-trout must have
been a three-pounder, and that will be reckoned a
big fish for Esk.

The ancient now leant his rod against the bridge

to execute some minor repairs, and was about to give me details of a wondrous catch of thirty years ago, when the air darkened and a warning dampness in the breeze sent me to seek shelter among the trees.

When I took the road again, my route was toward the great Burn Moor. The Willan, which I had to cross, is a rivulet of moods. Generally its bed is occupied by a succession of verdure-hid, deep, clear pools, joined by narrow gurgling ribbons of water; but now there issued from its granite dell a mighty surge of sound, and the flickering of a waterfall through the trees behind the cluster of houses called Boot caused me to turn aside. Down a great elbow of rock the rivulet was dashing. Here a creamy spout shot from some hidden cleft clear of the cliff, and crashed to spray on the boulders far below. This protruding slab of mossy rock a thin film of water tardily welled over. The harebell so precariously anchored to that ledge is hidden from sight; perhaps a stalk or two will be plucked away by the rude stream. Yet when Willan retires to seek its wonted way, nodding bells of azure blue will again uprear, a little bespattered with foam, yet perfect and strong, held into that hospitable cleft. But the main fosse is a little to the right. In three leaps it comes down fifty feet, throwing up a spume which is tinted by the sunbeams into a halo of rainbow hue. A few minutes later, as I passed up the steep mountain road, I turned for another look at Eskdale, the home of torrent. Great regiments of larches clothe the southern hills; the other side is festooned in green of fern and grass. From seaward the hills rise bolder and more rugged, with offshooting castles of jagged rocks overstanding the dale, with rifted gullies and gnarled woods where

> 'with sparkling foam a small cascade
> Illumines, from within, the leafy shade.'

Like a silver streak, the Esk wanders down the centre of the dale, with here and there dwindled cots and farms and fields and kine beside. A duskiness, forerunner of another stormlet, sweeps along, dimming the lustre of water and moist land. The sky is streaked with stretching pennons of rain-cloud, and I—I, with ne'er a cape to protect me—am standing on a bleak fell-track, far from shelter. I am neither hero nor philosopher to accept trials kindly, but I strongly wished to reach Windermere at nightfall, so heeded less the drenching shower. Care for health—the young are proverbially careless ; but if, when your clothes are completely saturated, you never allow your body to lose its temperature, a wetting more or less need not appal you. For years used to such inconvenience, I can only add that this theory is also practice with me.

Ere the top of the ascent was reached, the brief splashing shower had rushed on into the mountains. Across the cleft of the dale, right opposite me, from an unseen distance of moorland, a mighty torrent was pouring over the edge of a precipice. This was Birker Force.

> 'Resistless, roaring, dreadful, down it comes
> From the rude mountain and the mossy wild,
> Tumbled through rocks abrupt, and sounding far.'

The air was filled with the varied voices of many waters : gurglings from the near-at-hand springs and runnels; tinklings from the rivulets dropping down narrow rifts in the moor ; the rattle of the torrent speeding down the centre of the upland declivity ; and a dull, insistent roar carried up to the heights from the Willan cascade, the rock-racked Esk, and it might be from the far-away water-cloud of Birker.

My track across the moor was a bit inconsequent : sheep-tracks and man-tracks, anything trending in the right direction, were followed. Of course, the long tracts of bog had to be avoided—water oozed from them as from a huge sponge. In addition to these places, the whole moor was full of springs. Among the roots of heather were many up-currents, some with orifices six inches square; and their volumes spouted out with force, too, jets nearly a foot high being common. Had not my boots been filled long ago with the drops brushed from heather and bracken, I might have avoided these fountains, but under the circumstances I recked but little. Wide sheets of water were pouring down every slack, and I waded such as they were met. At one point from a pile of boulders I counted fifteen springs within ten feet.

Just as another crash of rain came along I sighted Burnmoor Tan. An old poacher of my acquaintance holds this water in high esteem; the trout are big and easily caught, he says. I have not tried the place: the fishing is private.

Standing by the darkling waters a splendid view is around. Wastwater Screes raise a green boundary to the left, to the right the ridges rise to Great Howe, and finally to Scawfell. An easy route up the last-named mountain is well in sight. A great pyramid of cloud rests beyond Wastdale, the dusky gulfs of Black Sail and Mosedale alone being seen below it. My route for the present lay straight ahead, over the narrow hause toward Wastdale. Twenty minutes on I am at the summit. A bright blaze of sunshine lights up Wastwater and the great circle of silurian rocks around it. In the level valley the eye first catches the yews, and then the modest gray church. This is the smallest in England. The conundrum and boast of a Wastdalian, when asked his birthplace, is : ' Ah cum fra whar there's t' hee'ist moontain, deepest lake, lilest kirk, an' t' biggest leer in aw England ' [I come from where there is the highest mountain, the deepest lake, the smallest church, and the biggest liar in all England]. But the sound of a foxhound's voice, shrill as of a pleased puppy, carries my mind to men rather than views—to Will Ritson and the old Parson. I have a story of these two, not new, and perhaps incomplete, which appertains at least to Wastdale. Many years ago a wandering fox played particular havoc among the flocks. Guns and dogs failing to close his account, one Sunday morning a party of dalesmen assaulted the earth he lay in with terrier and crowbar. However, while they attacked the front, Reynard escaped by a side-channel, and was speeding away for a securer home, when an alarm was raised. Collie and bobtail, hound and terrier, streamed across the hillside in pursuit. The fox headed for Mickledore, and was crossing at great speed the level fields near the church, when a worshipper— this happened in the days of long sermons—taking a mid-service stroll, raised a wild ' Tallyho!' and rushed back into the church, shouting : ' Here's t'

Ennerdale girt dog chasing for its life.' The droning homily from the pulpit was instantly lost in the clatter of clogs on the flagged floor, as pell-mell the congregation—men, women, and children —rushed out to join in the pursuit. If the parson sighed at this abandonment of the service, he did it in brief time, for a moment later his surplice was hanging on the pulpit-rail and he far afield, labouring to catch up his parishioners. Down with the fox! then and now, is the watchword of fells shepherding.

Some short distance I descended toward the vale; then, calculating that the time in hand allowed me to take an alternative course over Scawfell Pike, I deflected from the path and faced the wearisome side of Lingmell. As I rose higher my view seaward widened, and beyond the yellow sands of the Cumbrian coast I could see here and there a steamer shaping its course. Of course, the air was preternaturally clear, and even minute points came up sharply. Just as I climbed the last wall, a little man in homespun came along the upper track. I spoke to him, and he told me he was out ' looking his sheep.' Many of them had been affected by 't' wicks,' and he had had an anxious time, accordingly. 'But,' he added, 'it's nowt to what feeding them in winter time is for clash [wet weather] and hard work.' I asked him if he had ever been caught in a snowstorm while in charge of sheep. 'No,' he replied, 'and I don't want to. The fells here are that full of rocks and cliffs that it's dangerous work groping about in a thick snowshower.' Remembering an experience of my own not three miles from this, when a squall of January's whitest enveloped us without a minute's warning, I agreed. Only good luck brought us out of that incident happily, for every landmark was either deep under snow or hidden by the murkiness prevailing. The shepherd told of searches by lantern-light for missing neighbours ; no harm to life or limb had befallen any that he knew of, though the perils had been often great. Sometimes, he said, benighted tourists had to be sought for, but usually such were easily traced.

After walking about half a mile with me, my companion excused himself, saying that his flock lay towards Lord's Rake, on the other side of the brawling torrent. A few whistles and arm-swayings, and his two dogs were running far away, routing out stragglers from among the rocks and driving an ever-increasing band of sheep forward and upward. I followed the stony track to the top of Lingmell, and across a peat-stained expanse toward the last pitch of Scawfell Pike. A low cloud, distended and black with rain, had swept along and swamped out of sight the region ahead of me. I had reached the edge of the mist, when the thought of keeping level along the hillside struck me. I was now about 2,800 feet above sea-level, within 500 feet of the summit, and my proposed traverse was a new piece of work to me. From the top of the ridge you can see little of this abrupt slope ; from the bottom the detail of its facets and slacks is lost.

Huge splinters of stone lay on all sides, fragments which had fallen from above, and over these I clambered. Again and again I sidled along a narrow streaming ledge, steep rock above, a long gap below. Then the cloud began to shed rain in tremendous bursts, and the rocks became slippery. Once or twice I ventured along routes which, though promising at first, became impassable, and I had to get back to my starting-point as I could. When the stormlet was at its strongest there was suddenly from above a sharp rapping sound—like the reports of a Maxim gun—some little distance away. Five seconds or so the sound lasted ; there was a brief pause as though the world of rigid stone and driving rain hung in the balance, then a magnificent crash of thunder seemed to make the rock veins start and quiver. The mighty sound came from a lower level, and I heard it re-echoing up the glen to Styehead, with many a back-

ward-flung cadence. The play of lightning through
the mist-wreaths was splendid. There was another
roll of heaven's-war drum as I picked my way
across upper Piers Ghyll. How that great chine
seemed to hold the sound, buffeting it from cliff to
cliff, from foaming beck to lowering cloud! At last
I judged it meet to turn my face up the hill, hoping
to come near the path where the Esk springs from
a small marsh. In ten minutes I was within earshot
of a party of climbers, surprising them somewhat
as I stepped through the curling mist almost into
their midst.

IV. A Sketch of Duddonside

At the stepping-stones people on wandering bent generally cross, and, turning upstream, are soon within the mighty Duddon gorge, where founts of green water dash through barriers of piled-up rocks crowned with heather and brambles.

It was early autumn. Through the cool air came the notes of some of the later songsters, on the moors beds of green bracken still waved, but here and there single fronds were turning orange and crimson and yellow. Great bushes of glossy holly began to be noticeable on the crags as the brakes of hazel and whitethorn thinned off their summer foliage. On the bosky hillsides whitish patches of sphagnum were framed with bands of fiery red bog-grass. The dale was resonant to the turmoilings of water, down every ghyll foaming cataracts sprang, while here and there deep floods surged through the level woodlands. The air was marvellously clear, every knot and slack on the mountains showed plainly, and the fresh

bright sunshine gave everything, from the caërn
on the topmost crag of Wallabarrow to the wind-
tangled bracken-beds near our path, a halo of
glory. Here and there rabbits frisked to the
shelter of burrow or fern, and once the half-choke
of a cock-pheasant called his harem together to
flee our approach. Along a path marked with pools
of mud and water and studded with boulders we
plunged into the low screen of oak and ash, and
in a few minutes were beside the stepping-stones.

The river in front was at half-flood ; the crossing
was covered a foot deep with clear, racing water.
Far upstream, waterbreaks were gleaming between
gray boulders and many-tinted coppices ; the roar
as the current fretted through its rough channel
came to our ears incessantly. In the shade of the
larches we found an almost level path to our left,
worn, doubtless, by sheep ranging the glades of
these woods. A jay screamed and flew away, its
blue side-feathers attracting the eye as it winged
through the maze of stems. The river was again
close beside—a deep pool in which the sunlit water
seemed to collect strength to go babbling down an
inclined beach of smoothed stones. The river-bank
became tangled with brambles and dense coppice,
so we turned into a mysterious hollow where
perhaps centuries ago Duddon's stream varied
from its present bed. In a few yards we cleared

the trees and stood by a hollow in the woods.
The stream in its ancient course had here tarried
awhile and delved out a circular pool before
passing seaward. Here, perhaps, the red deer
had come by moonlight to drink—I never ramble
by Duddonside without my memory reverting
to these animals, which less than a century ago
roamed in wild freedom over the great silent
wastes surrounding the valley. But now the
bracken is rustled by wandering sheep, which turn
and stare at such unusual visitors. We fringed
this eddying place of a forgetful river, and dived
into the dense coppice beyond, where brambles so
hampered our path that we left the proximity of
the water to find an old cart-track. On the hazel
bushes a few nuts still hung, and twice there were
glimpses of flying russet and white — squirrels
disturbed at their repast. The old 'gait' found,
we strolled steadily along: this wood in springtime
must have been carpeted with blue ; the fleshy
green leaves of the bluebell protrude through
layers of rotting leaves and twigs. But when
autumn is at hand flowers are rare in the riverside
woods—a solitary strawberry bloom, maybe, with
here and there a belated primrose or daisy. What
the sweet summer glory of this paradise has been
is recalled by the wealth of dead honeysuckle
trailers and the dried-up stems of many wild-

vines. Now, descending a sharp hillock, we are by the ford in Tarn beck. The steady murmur to our right warns us of near Duddon, and we resolve to walk down to where the waters meet. The saplings are so dense by the waterside that we again seek the less difficult woods, coming at last to a narrow path bounded by thorn-bushes, brambles, and the punishing boughs of the wild-rose-tree. Ten yards on we are on the point where the two streams meet. Tarn beck has scooped itself a little bay, but the lordly Duddon here sleeps in a deep pool among the shingles.

What words can describe the contrast between the rattling, dashing rivulet and the great placid, sunlit stream into which it falls and is lost? On this very spot, amid a tangle of brambles and many fronded brackens, the great poet of the fells stood in imagination when he wrote :

> 'Duddon . . .
> Who, 'mid a world of images imprest
> On the calm depth of his transparent breast,
> Appears to cherish most that Torrent white,
> The fairest, softest, liveliest of them all.'

He saw it at 'the busy hum of noon,' when its 'murmur musical' promised refreshment to distant meadows needing rain; but what would he have written if he had seen it as we did, if he had seen the velvet green of the aftermath in the fields across the river, and noted the woods of autumn just flushing into realms of red and crimson and gold—if he had witnessed the glory of that October morning, when the air was instinct with light, and the ear was charmed with varied cadences of falling and rippling water? Then Wordsworth's magic pen would have traced lines fairer far than those the scene actually inspired. But, alas! the mind of a trifler with Nature rises with difficulty to such enchanted heights nor stays there—for cunningly hid between the veiling undergrowth and the upspringing grass I espied the stem of a sapling ash with its branchlets roughly lopped off. For curiosity I drew this forth, and, lo! there, scraped on the tender gray-green bark, here and there— bitten through to the white wood—were the marks of the rings attached to the salmon-poacher's bag- net. Wordsworth and the serene majesty of the morning were alike instantly forgotten in the contemplation of this sign of a 'black art.' It was simple enough to conjure up that scene of last night.

About a dozen salmon have collected in this pool, waiting for a flood to allow them to pass through the roaring, broken rapids of the gorge to spawning redds far above. For some hours vigilant eyes have been upon their movements, and now in the pitch darkness of midnight two men approach the riverside from opposite directions. Cautious signals are exchanged ere they meet behind a screen of bushes, and are repeated as they stealthily patrol the riversides. Then away in the woods near the stepping-stones the axe is plied with muffled vigour ; the branches rustle with their neighbours as, the stem being severed, they are drawn downward. The steel is scarcely audible as the lesser limbs are struck away and the net-pole prepared. With hardly a sound the poacher threads his way through the coppices, and he is soon again by the pool's marge.

In the meantime his comrade has drawn their net from beneath the concave bank, has laid it straight on the dank grass (there is the draggled, tramped sward), and soon has the rings fixed on the pole. Now all is ready, and the younger man takes the long shaft, and with a sweep draws the net into the pool. In a moment it becomes saturated and sinks, then is carefully drawn forward. The strain on the netsman is great ; he bends to the task and puts forward his utmost strength, but in vain. He cannot force his contrivance against the current—here, though flowing soft, Duddon is really very powerful—so his comrade comes to his assistance.

By their united efforts the net is brought nearer land. As they bend over, the sheen from the water lights up the faces of the struggling men.

There is satisfaction in every coarse and bloated line. As the net moves the surface of the pool becomes troubled, a fin or a tail cuts through the water: the salmon, though enmeshed, are exerting themselves to escape. But in vain, for, with an oath at the coldness of the water, the elder poacher steps into the pool, going deeper and deeper till the water rises to his shoulders, till he is able to force the pole and its heavily-laden bag-net to the surface and then ashore. In the clear depths his footmarks are traceable by the places where the moss was scraped from the stones by the hobnails of his boots.

The fish are rapidly killed and their carcases placed in bags (here and there a broken scale gleams silvern among the grass and shales); then, one carrying the unrigged net in addition to his load of salmon, the poachers are quickly lost to sight in the woods. Such is the story told by the abandoned net-pole and the shores of the robbed salmon-pool.

We turned aside from the river, scrambling up a steep clay bank, forcing a passage through a barricade of hazels, and in a couple of minutes were once again in a cleared area. Crossing this, in the shadow of the larch grove, here and there were quite considerable conical mounds, seemingly composed of dead sections of twigs. In and out of these by a thousand tunnel entrances were moving files of large black ants. These hills claimed our attention awhile. They were indeed cunningly built, and more than once a longing came to make an examination of their interiors. A scientist or a competent naturalist would have been justified in such an experiment, but not a pair of mere wanderers.

To compensate us, as it seemed, almost at once we heard a soft patter of paws and a soughing of delicate branches—a squirrel was dashing along the boughs not far away. As soon as the tree-bole was reached, the russet body whisked out of sight at great speed, but an eye kept on the point where it disappeared soon detected two sharp, tufted ears and a pair of bright eyes anxiously watching our movements. I called my companion's attention to this, and so long as we refrained from movement the keen three-sided contemplation went on ; but as soon as my arm stirred the little head was withdrawn, and I knew that four legs were carrying the squirrel swiftly up towards the crown of the tree. And, as anticipated, after the lapse of a few seconds the little animal reappeared on a branch quite a long way up, quietly observing us. The squirrels of Duddonside suffer little persecution by humans evidently, for this one had a curious, if rather

distant, interest in us, and refused to be scared by
any pretence at hostilities. Even as we moved
away, a backward glance told us that the animal
had altered its position to get a final glance, and
was now hanging head downwards, peering at us
from *under* the branch it was sitting upon.

A few minutes more, and the swiftly-moving
waters of Duddon appear through the straight
larch-stems. We are close beside the impassable
stepping-stones and our path back from the woods
to the little hamlet by the church.

V. Ghyll-climbing

NEARLY the most miserable class in society contains those who have just fallen below distinction, while their efforts have raised them high above mediocrity. These persons are unjustly described by the brilliant as 'the rank and file.'

In crag-climbing there are a few who seem to successfully emulate a fly or a spider in negotiating slippery rock walls, who can scramble unmoved along the sheerest precipices, or climb untiringly at the steepest ascents. Then come 'the rank and file,' whose deficiency of nerve or strength does not permit such risky work. Where do we find this class during the holiday season? Squatting under some towering crag, maybe, which it is their ambition to ascend, in the vain hope that familiarity with its outline will breed contempt for its dangers. Or spread - eagled in some dangerous situation, as the man who many years ago attempted to climb Piers Ghyll, a narrow, deep chasm in the side of Scawfell Pike (Cumberland). He scrambled to a ledge nearly level with the waterfall which closes the direct ascent of this most majestic ghyll, then lost confidence, and dared neither advance nor retreat. Twenty-four hours' exposure made him desperate enough to leap into the fall pool thirty feet beneath, in which manner he escaped.

'A good cragsman is a good mountaineer' is a proved axiom; but when the fells are so thoroughly and accurately mapped out, and paths are so distinctly traceable as they now are, few adventures happen to the careful man, and the fierce struggles which form the chief delight of crag-climbing are woefully lacking.

There is another branch of British fellscraft, however, which may meet with the favour of such persons, and which should be better known to everyone. But to discuss this it must be assumed that every climbing-machine, every rock-scrambler, has found his natural sport, for the man to whom this pastime is open must be able to discern grace and symmetry in the water-hewn rocks, picturesqueness in the beetling crags, and lively interest in the many charms of the ghylls of the fells.

A ghyll, it may be explained, is the hacked-out course of a fell, beck, or stream, and may be divided into three scenic sections: First, the approach, generally by a wide moorland glen, narrowing into a defile at its head, and choked with boulders of all sizes and shapes. The succeeding portion is the gully proper. The deepest waterfalls are here, as is also the hardest climbing. The lofty cliffs surrounding the fosse are split into irregular chimneys, yards wide rise spray-washed slabs without the slightest irregularity on their polished surfaces. The head of the ghyll is a return to the natural scenery of the fell. In some places this is reached by an easy grass ascent, in others after a rough scramble over piled fragments of rock.

A steep cornice may, however, bar the way, or the ghyll debouch into the hollow of a scree basin. Then comes a struggle upwards ; the grit slides away at every step. The wide scree gully in which the stream of débris originates is reached, and progress becomes not a little dangerous. The rotten 'mountain delight' which your feet have set in motion slips away from loose rocks on the higher slopes, and down they bound at fearful rates. Keep in the shelter if you can, and wait for the solid rain to cease. You cannot dodge the flying pieces, for, however quick your eye may be in marking, the treacherous foothold does not permit rapid movement. And the speed some of these dislodged stones attain is wonderful. The writer remembers, when climbing a scree under Fairfield, seeing a portion of cliff topple over some hundred feet in front. It simply bounced through the air, struck a spur from the parent rock some dozen yards from him, and burst into dust and splinters. The crash was louder than the explosion of a fair-sized cannon, and the very mountain seemed to quiver at the shock. Had not a crevice afforded shelter from the mass of shingle which for some ten minutes whistled down the slope, these lines would never have been written.

Some ghylls are mere fissures in the mountainsides, with lofty cliffs rising sheer from their beck beds. In these the imprisoned water races down without a break on its surface, a yard wide, perhaps four deep. You scramble along the wall of rock and look down upon the scene, or laboriously work a way along the ledges, at every turn leaping the stream, leaving insecure foot and hand hold on one side for points equally insecure on the other. Then you come to a cataract; the brook tumbles over an abrupt rock into the deep and narrow basin, hollowed by and for itself. The gorge is closed; advance is at an end, retreat impossible, for there is not room on the narrow ledge in which to face about.

There against the skyline, forty feet or more

up, is a splinter of harder rock which has separated itself from the cliff. Follow its bold outline to the water, where it forms the promontory between two minute bays. A tiny crack shows in the angle at the head of the cove, up which is the only way out; but there are five yards of mossy, damp crag between you and that. Carefully the body is pressed against the slippery surface, and a sidle forward commences, a notch, a microscopic chink affording precarious hold. The tiny bay is reached, and a few feet further is the crevice desired. An outcrop of felspar now forms a tiny escarpment above your head, and, holding to this, you drag along the sheer smooth breast of rock, your whole weight on your arms. If the ledge presents the slightest irregularity, your fingers will fail to grasp it, and down with a mighty splash you go into the dimpling pool. But the worst predicament is not eternal, and in ten seconds you have got into the cranny. After a short breather, up the chimney you struggle, wrist, forearm, thigh, and calf, all working at their fullest power. A gathering light comes in from the left through the cleft between the narrow crag and the cliff. A lightning flash, more powerful than wind or weather, has cracked the former in many places, making it dangerous to ascend. The platform behind, however, affords foothold, and you have another welcome rest. The roar of the waterfall fills your ears, and you look through the gap at it. How curiously near it seems!—you can almost step into its creamy spout. Splash, splash, thud, crunch—splash, splash, thud, crunch, in wearying reiteration comes up from the well below. Across the gulf a sheer cliff rises, lined and broken in its upper part as its twin on which you are clinging, but dropping, a broad smooth slab, into the whirlpool of the force beneath.

In other ghylls the climbing is less severe— these are the pretty, secluded glens by which the effluent of many a mountain tarn finds its way to the parent river. The first two miles of the one in mind are between bracken-covered slopes. Willows, mountain-ashes, and hollies flourish; the clear water rushes down rock-slides from pool to pool. But further up the scenery becomes wilder. The bed of the beck is strewn with large fragments of rock fallen from aloft, which are happily adapted to the many-shaped waterfalls displayed in the first short gully. There is some hazard in frequenting these places, as many a man has had proof. The shepherd has possibly seen the fall of an immense mass of rock into the shallow where a day or two previously his charge made halt to drink. I know one ghyll which in a single night was choked by the fall of a neighbouring cliff, so that a lovely waterfall was formed, with a deep pool above and another below the obstruction. Many a natural bridge of 'chocked' rock is formed by such an event. In the higher portion of this stream is a large tarn, and just before it is sighted the waters of the outflow are pent into a gorge between two mountains, and cascade after cascade breaks upon the view. Climb along the river-bed here; it is difficult and toilsome work, but the vantage is unique. The water churns round in a mad whirlpool here; a few yards in front it races towards us on what appears to be one lofty rock-shoot, but which discovers itself into a dozen separate falls. The water does not seem to fall from one to another of these; it is more of a single roll or a bound. Alert, bright trout dart about in transparent water, devouring whatever food the beck brings down—a hard-cased bracken clock which has attempted a flight beyond its power and perished, a soft mollusc torn from its rock home, or a caterpillar dislodged by the passing breeze from some twig.

Carefully coasting round a mossy corner into a recess from which the cheerful thunder of water proceeds, we enter a crag basin of remarkable charm. We find footing on a slab which almost spans the stream. It has peeled from the cliff above, and has been caught in its descent on a narrow ledge. The brook plashes against its sides, and grumbles under it to the outlet. The spray-damped cliffs are green with moss; down the gaps by which the springs from above reach their bourne hang long streamers of water-weed; a wren has taken possession of a dry pocket among the rocks opposite, and is surveying us suspiciously. It twitters and scolds, defies and threatens, but its trouble is for nothing. The niche in which it homes is impossible to reach, even if we were so minded. Green and gray and yellow, white and crimson and brown, are imparted to the drier precipices by the lichens; silvery birch boughs sway above, green-yellow roots hang into the turmoil of the water. A dipper dashing up the gully sees a human presence, hesitates a flash, then passes at accelerated speed, its wild song echoing over the drone and boom without a tremor or a pause. This rock hollow is merely one among many equally pretty, and pen, pencil, or brush fail to convey half its delights.

As the slippery cliffs afford no handhold on this side, we cross the slab, and attack a cleft down which dangle, as so many ropes, the roots of a mountain-ash. Holding to these, we easily gain the higher level of the glen, and make forward. Passing the mountain tarn, we enter the upper col; and among my many climbs, this has been the most unsatisfactory. It is a wild delve in the mountainside; steep banks of scree slope into it, with here and there a tongue-like bank of tawny grass.

The little stream purls and rattles by your side as you force your way over the yielding débris, promising a rocky and picturesque source. Higher and higher you struggle, and the water correspondingly shrinks in volume. The fanlike streams of shale and dust have here invaded the narrow dell, and you may hear the beck grumbling and spouting beneath the feet. Further up the ground seems to rise more abruptly, and your hopes rise, to be quickly dashed, for the stream is now too weak to burrow a course for itself. The moisture from a wide grassy basin percolates through dank green moss, tinkles in thin lines down the inequalities, or in wide glassy sheets slides—it cannot be said to flow—among the steeper rock-faces, accommodating itself to all angles without a sound or a splash. And this is the source of the stream you have so laboriously traced.

Another fine gully is entered from an old quarry. After carefully negotiating a succession of dripping slabs, on hands and knees, you reach the darkened bed of a chasm. On the right the

light is excluded by perpendicular rocks, crowned
with a plantation of dark firs; on the left a less
abrupt slope, covered with dainty oak-fern and
evil-smelling 'ramps,' rises to a thicket of hazel,
overtopped by ash saplings. A couple of these
have fallen and form a living bridge high above
the stream. Climb carefully here, and shun the
ferny slope, for the thin bed of leaf-mould slides
down with the slightest pressure. A misty gleam
in front shows that the chasm widens; the noise
of falling water proclaims a cataract, and soon its
trough is reached. The tiny stream is descending
a succession of mossy steps, now close to one
bank, now to the other, wandering as it wills over
the wide face of rock. In winter, when the spongy
fell is thoroughly saturated, a huge volume crashes
through this defile. Then the gorge is impossible
to scale, the trough is a churn of angry, yellow-
brown waters, and the tiny tinkle deepens to a
majestic roar. Above the fall the water still
descends in picturesque cascades, at one moment
rushing pell-mell down a tiny crevice between
smooth black rocks, playfully diving into a deep
black dub at another. In one corner it divides
round a green boulder, on which a few wisps of
grass and a foxglove find sustenance; further up
it passed an abrupt ledge in a pretty spout. The
merriment of the brook seems to infect you, and

you feel that you have lost a companion when you
reach its source in the

> ' Mere of the moorland,
> Boulder-environed.'

Entering another ravine which has a most unpromising opening near the top of a slate-quarry,
we notice stupendous crags which augur hard
work. Their lower strata are, however, much
broken, and the first emerald-green basin of water
is easily passed ; but further up a giant mass over-
hangs the ghyll. After carefully surveying both
sides, a tiny jut is tried and found wanting. The
adventurer loses hold on the rock and is immediately immersed in about ten feet of water. The
other bank is examined more carefully, and a long
traverse discovered. Along this we warily sidle,
making holds for hands where possible. At a
most awkward point the traverse comes to an
end, and the way back has to be crawled at some
risk.

The most dangerous gully incident was met
when climbing by a waterfall. The rock (ironstone) was steep, but rotten. We directed our
climb towards a block apparently about five feet
in diameter. Perhaps this was finely poised on a
bed of yielding sand or clay, for as soon as we got
weight upon it over it toppled, narrowly missing
crushing us against the wall. The boulder fell

into the deep water, and, of course, we fell too. A wetting was a lucky finish to this adventure.

I well remember descending a very pretty ghyll —or was it the splendid conditions which made it so? It was a lovely morning, and we had climbed Kentmere High Street during the hours of dusk in order to see the sun rise. A long bank of purple haze had lain along the horizon, but the sun rapidly rose above this and flooded hill and valley, mountain and lake, in a very blaze of glory. At 5.30 we made a move towards Mardale, where we hoped to get some breakfast. Down the steep mountain-shoulder, where the path dodged among the boulders, we made rapid progress to Blea Water, the waters of which were rippling in a slight breeze. At the foot of the tarn we sat for awhile on the gray lichened slabs, enjoying the bright, warm morning sunshine. Then down the bracken-covered slope again to a small waterfall most picturesquely situated. The sun shone directly into its deep rocky basin, and every surge of the tumbling water was telegraphed to the eye in flash and glitter. Some mountain-ash-trees clung round the steep rock, their long roots, white and green, hanging dripping into the clear pool below. Seen under these indescribable circumstances, the sight was a very memorable one. It was only the pangs of hunger that forced us to move on.

One of the best expeditions for one who has a real liking for the smaller beauties of water and rock scenery is to Sacgill. This is at the head of Longsleddale, a long narrow valley of the usual Lakeland type, with an unusually cramped defile at the foot. Right in front, as you cross the narrow switchback bridge from the cluster of antiquated houses known as Sacgill, and turn up the edge of the torrent, are Harter Fell and Gray Crag, the abrupt front of the former continuing in Goat Scar, a pile of rough, fox-haunted crags. As the walk is proceeded with, a curious depression in the dalehead is reached—a flat entirely covered with stone, which at some distant time has evidently been a small tarn. Portions of this level are still banked up to make pools for sheep-washing, and a strong wall has been built across at the foot to prevent the loose débris washing at flood-time on the cultivated valley below. At the head of the depression comes our ghyll. At first the usual succession of small cataracts, each with its clear pool where the water swirls awhile ere escaping down the water-worn green slabs which constitute the steep river-bed. The path, or, rather, the sheep-track which serves this purpose, becomes steeper, and the falls correspondingly higher. You rise from the valley in a succession of mighty steps; the shelf on which you are standing prevents your seeing the route by which you came, giving in return a distant view of the valley shimmering in the bright sunshine, with, still further, range after range of moorish hills, with, here and there a rough cliff, till the distant sea closes the view.

You are now in the very jaws of the pass; a spur of Goat Scar approaches the stream from the left, and a tall corner of Gray Crag forces itself into the narrowing glen opposite. Now the more immediate river-banks rise higher, the rolling waters in front come by a swiftly descending curve. At this point we climb round the foot of the rocky bank, here some fifty feet high, and find a standing-place on a small beach. This is the only place in the rock basin where such a foothold is possible. Behind us the crags rise, covered with tiny clumps of mountain-sage, and fringed at their tops with waving bracken fronds. Beyond, higher and higher, rise the stony ridges to the crags, which strike the eye in whichever direction it is turned. The beck tumbles into the small cleft, and as yet its unbroken descent is out of sight, but the soft, liquid, churning sound betrays its presence.

As other venues fail us, a tough scramble up the grass-hung bank commences. From the bank of the gorge are several grand vertical views through luxuriant mountain-ashes of the stream dimpling in the deep crevice, and then of the waterfall, with its brink twenty feet beneath, its chasm fully fifty. Further on come a number of pretty cascades; then you emerge from a water-hewn gallery on a level with the stream. As the pass widens, a belt of tough slaty rocks is approached, and down these the beck shoots. Not a bush grows near—we are at too high an elevation—and the view savours of desolation. Damp, green rocks pall; the succession of streams sliding almost noiselessly down long smooth surfaces becomes monotonous; ridge after ridge of stony fells give a dreary impression. But just where the pass opens into the swampy moor is its redeeming feature. Threading along the course of the beck, we see a stream issuing from a crag-guarded ghyll, and on approach find that the stream fills it from bank to bank. A few stepping-stones allow one to reach a place where some advance can be made along the foot of the cliffs. Then ford the stream at the shallow, and climb the jutting crag to the right. You are now in an amphitheatre of rocks. In front is the waterfall, its spray damping you through; almost beneath is the chinklike passage through which the water escapes. On either hand tall crags rise, all dripping with spray and hung with luxuriant mosses. Here and there a fern—hart's-tongue or similar slime-loving variety—finds root-hold; a huge fragment, torn down, maybe, by lightning, reclines precariously in a corner, ready, it seems, to fall and block up the pool. An active person can spring easily across the narrow gulf to the cliff over which the stream is pouring, and there find sufficient hold to climb out. But it allows of no mistakes. A fall into the well of the cascade is to be dreaded, as the unfortunate could only trust to the stream carrying him into the outflow passage; there is no handhold within reach by which a good position could be secured again. After this ghyll, not more than fifty yards in length, has been explored, the tour is finished, and it cannot fail to have been a most pleasing one.

VI. Mountain Moonlight

EVENING drew on apace as we walked out of
Keswick by the Castlehead road. The ground,
though not frozen, was firm and dry, and the
faint breeze carried just a tinge of winter from
northward. In the great hollow behind us lights
began to twinkle here and there. Lake Bassenthwaite stetched like a sheet of blue steel between
the steep slopes of Skiddaw and the brown coppices beneath Barf, while the cloudless western
sky still glowed with the waning radiance of
sunset.

On the hills lingered day; in the valleys night
was nigh. At a corner in the long ascent we
paused. A thin blue mist was gradually ascending,
extending and joining into a canopy beneath which
the lowlands were rapidly lost to view. Two wide
fleecy clouds showed where the lakes lay. The
vapour rising from the Derwent marked a streak
across the level meadows between them; a thousand rills sent up their several lines to make a

pall over the wide Newlands Vale, while a reek-like smoke rose from where Greta fretted over its deep rocky course beneath Latrigg. Ere we finally turned away, our eyes had wandered for some minutes over a continuous, slowly-moving sea of cloud, upon which the solid fells and precipitous crags seemed to be floating.

In half an hour we had crossed the ridge of Castlerigg. Through the leafless hedgerows bounding our track to the right a series of dark summits approached us closely. The last glare of day had left the sky, and above these rugged heights shone a few of the brighter lamps of heaven. A dull cloak of vapour occupied the hollowness in front, with the stumpy Naddle fell standing islandwise, for beyond it could be seen the night mists o'erhanging St. John's Vale. To our left Blencathra was the most prominent mountain, its huge mass and sharp, broken contour showing to great advantage in the starlight, while along the eastern horizon stood the leviathan Helvellyn range, some five miles away.

A pale primrose light ran along their topmost ridge, flushing the sky so that for a space the sparkling stars could not be seen. The moon, we knew, was about to rise ; indeed, we had chosen this night for a stroll because continuous light would illumine our way. It was grand walking along that hardened road, watching for rifts in the drifting mist above us, giving us brief glimpses of the brightening quarter of the sky. But we were within the shade of the mighty mountains before the moment arrived when the moon would appear over Crossfell, and flood with bright, uncertain light the upper world of mountains. But instead of this spectacle we watched, as we groped up the pony-track in the semi-darkness, the light touch the summits, and then the narrow ' edges,' or ridge-approaches, to Blencathra, making every boulder and cranny on the eastward side visible, accentuating the steepness and ruggedness by leaving the western slopes in utter darkness.

Perhaps five minutes' walk below the crest of the pass we stopped to view the scene at leisure, and to regain our breath for the brief final ascent. To northward a great ridge of mountains, furrowed with dark ghylls and decked with great rock-faces and beds of scree ; beyond, the uncertain glimmer of lakes caught through riven masses of mist ; still further away (to westward), a sea of blue mountain - tops. To the right of these, broad moors and craggy fells, shadowy glens and sparkling tarns, with here and there a twinkling rivulet. But the finest scene of all was a crag deep beneath our feet, seemingly

'with airy turrets crowned,
Buttress, and rampire's circling bound,
And mighty keep and tower.'

With the level fleeces of mist kissing its lowest wall of slabs, it seemed a veritable castle suspended in mid-air, yet so real that we seemed to listen for the challenging blast of an Arthur's horn to shake the echoes of the hills upon which the solid pile of gray would once again rouse itself to life and light. But even in this hour of moonlit witchery our senses would not play us false, and carry us back in spirit to the fabled days of old.

We turned in silence to resume our journey, yet it was not with cold we drew that sharp breath. For on the bright skyline above us horses and men were moving. Knights-errant? No, they were not clad in glistering mail from top to toe, nor carried they the bows and spears of the men of the Border raids. No, they were peaceful farmers of Legburthwaite, returning from a sheep-fair in another vale. We greeted them warmly—Nature at its loveliest, as we see it to-night, yet makes a man feel lonesome—and after a few words they passed on. But for long their occasional voices and the ringing of the horseshoes on the stony track were companionable sounds.

We did not quite ascend to the top of the pass, but just as the eastward prospect began to open

turned southward for Helvellyn. There was no
path, but the ground was fairly even. A flank of
the great mountain cut off the view of dun,
coppice-fringed Thirlmere ; an outcrop beneath
our feet hid the Vale of St. John. There was
but little breeze on the uplands. The sound
of a prowling fox or the bark of a wakeful dog at
a sheep-farm in the gulf beneath again and again
came to our ears as we strode along the grassy
brae nearer to the highest peak.

'Now for a short rush': for thus years ago was
I introduced to the wonderful view, and I like to
re-feel when possible that glorious sensation. So
up to the crest we came. As we stood there in
the cold night air, it seemed to me that in a few
yards we had climbed into another world. Our
feet were upon a narrow beach of loose, clinking
mountain limestone. To right and left the ground
continued a few paces, then abruptly fell into
depths unseen, and beyond, at a much lower
elevation, the eye rested upon the jagged rocks
of Striding Edge and Catchedecam. That long
floating cloud is Ullswater. The confused masses
are raising themselves somewhat, and the narrow
waters of the lake in all their moonlit loveliness
are partially to be seen.

Every one of the deep abysses radiating from
the ridge on which we stand is occupied by a

wandering patch of white vapour, but, as often happens, the moist places have by this time ceased their supply, and the clouds are gradually thinning and will shortly disappear. We felt as though from some insecure, lofty platform we stood regarding the creation of a world of giant rocks. Everything seemed so huge, so primitive, so awe-inspiring. A patch of thin night mist could hide every vestige of men's handiwork ; but up here works of God's own fashioning stood supreme, overtowering the highest banks of vapour, and sheering in majestic silence their ambitious shoulders far up into the starlit sky.

For long we stood gazing—first north, to where the view ended on the plains of Cumberland ; southward, over enormous piles of rocks, and over mist-brimming hollows where we knew lakes were hid ; eastward, over a mass of mountains furrowed with deep valleys ; westward, over low moors to a silvery range of heights.

My eye was perhaps most attracted to a long and nearly level series of ridges, along which I knew the Romans of old had built a road which still endures. More than once I had walked there by moonlight, and noted the giant front of Helvellyn, fenced with crags and strewn with scree, formidable-looking even so far away. But the chill air of night compelled us to move, and for an hour along the crest we walked, skirting cliffs which fell away abruptly to pastoral coves, and coming at last to where over the dark Grisedale Tarn we came opposite the long scree-strewn shoulder of Fairfield.

The only sheep we met as we walked along the ridge was most palpably a 'stray.' When the flock were driven down from the heights a month ago, this item managed to avoid both dogs and shepherd. Poor creature! it hailed us with a loud bleat; but though we had wished to give it help, we knew not whither to drive it. What happens to such during winter? The ravens and hawks and foxes squabble over their carcases at the foot of deep cliffs they have wandered over during time of storm, or in the narrow ghylls where their bodies lie after the drift in which they were smothered has melted away. Sometimes also the sheep's wanderings are ended by a splinter of rock falling upon it as it threads the path beneath the precipices. A good many of the 'strays' are undeniably collected by the dread 'night-shepherds' —sheep-stealers. Anyhow, very few are folded home or met again when with spring the flocks return to the uplands.

Now we turned westward, traversing a bog from which a streamlet flowed, and by the descending course of this we quickly returned to the dale. From Sticks Pass to the bog we had walked six continuous miles without coming so low down as 2,000 feet above sea-level. The whole journey was within the region of barrenness. The ground was strewed with stones of various sizes, between which bent-grass and occasional mosses—and in summer a few hardy saxifrages and other alpine flowerets—made a show of life. Once the hoot of a wandering owl came up from a ravine in Nethermost Cove. Everthing winged had left the uplands on the approach of winter; the other migrants would come with the snow.

From Wythburn we crossed the fields to the west shore of Thirlmere. The moon had now risen high above the mountains, making a mellow path along the waters. It was delightful, and not too cold, to lean awhile on the wall next the road, look at the long ridge of mountain we had walked upon, and to watch the flocks of wild-duck and geese quickly moving about the moonlit bays at our feet. Midnight was past long before we neared Armboth, where the ghosts of the Lake Country families are said to meet and hold occasional revel, and in another two hours, after many a halt to enjoy the glory of the night, we were at that corner in the long Castlehead whence we watched day fade from the western sky. The valley beneath was still the haunt of floating mists ; at one moment there was a bewitching glimpse up Newlands Vale, at another we saw the silver moonlight streaming across Lake Bassenthwaite. Yet after our ramble of some twenty-six miles we were loath to go indoors, and first repaired to Friar's Crag, where perchance the cloud might rive apart and let us see Derwent Water in all its moonlit unearthly beauty, with its wooded islets floating like bits of paradise upon its tranquil bosom.

The clouds did open while we stood there. Words cannot convey what we saw.

THE DALESMEN'S SPORT

THE DALESMEN'S SPORT

Mountain Fox-hunting

Despite the difficulties presented by the rough surfaces and the peculiar weather associated with such elevations, fox-hunting is carried on to a large extent among the fells. The natives are sportsmen from their wild environment and the opportunities it gives for the chase. Foxes are too plentiful, their depredations being bewailed by every farmer, shepherd, and poultry-raiser within the area mentioned. The farm hands have comparatively little to do in winter, for the sheep are brought from the distant uplands on the approach of hard weather, and their attention, therefore, only takes up a few hours of each day. As the shepherd seldom, even on the darkest mornings, turns out later than five a.m., it will be readily understood that there is plenty of daylight left for hunting.

Four packs of hounds hunt the Lake Country, and, circumscribed though the area is, there is no difficulty in arranging meets. Appointments seldom clash, for each mountain group has its own foxes and earths, and it is only when they cannot get to earth near home that they rush away over miles of crag and grass, in the usually vain hope of outstripping their pursuers. Many years ago a fox made a circuitous route about the moors at the foot of Kentmere, then ran over into Long-sleddale, giving a good forty-five minutes round that valley before the kill. Two packs having joined in the chase, some discussion arose as to which should claim the fox. Two veteran dales-men were therefore appointed arbitrators, and arrived at a satisfactory decision by selecting the hounds which, in their opinion, had most distin-guished themselves in the later stages of the chase.

The hounds most adapted to this class of hunting are big, strong animals ; in no pack is uniformity a craze, either in colour or size. Most huntsmen keep a couple of small but exceedingly fast hounds, as they can help the terriers in some of the wider tunnels in the earths, where occasionally a fox will lie at bay on a rock-shelf out of reach of its smaller pursuers. These terriers are very small, hard animals, pugnacious in their excitement but wonderfully docile both before and after. They cannot, of course, pass the rough country at the speed of hounds—barely can they keep up with the humans; therefore the huntsman frequently gives them a lift in his capacious side-pockets. The memories of some of the terriers are phenomenal; only let the pack drive their fox into a particular hole, and its location and interior arrangements are indelibly fixed in the little dogs' minds.

The life of a fells fox does not present many new features; from birth he has to exert all his marvellous instincts for self-preservation. In spring and summer he lies out for days on the open moors, where the huntsmen dare not come, for fear of injuring the ewes and lambs. All summer Reynard is the scourge of the fells, but when wintry days cover his usual haunts with snow, he is forced to leave for the valleys. 'Circling round the top of Bowfell were twelve ravens, uttering their hoarse cries, and diving persistently towards some object among the rocks. The safety of their carrion breakfast was at stake, for a prowling fox was evidently the butt at which they were worrying. As we neared the summit, a deep gully on the Langdale side, full of snow and with a considerable cornice at the top, showed where Reynard had escaped his tormentors. The white mantle of snow was covered with the footmarks of the birds, and backwards and forwards along the very edge of the precipice the fox had passed and repassed, evidently afraid to make the plunge. An overhanging rock upon the left, where the snow lay at a severe angle, had given the chance he sought, and he had jumped over, going up to the hips in the fluffy drift beneath.'

By this season the packs are again on the alert, and only occasionally are the foxes given a rest. At a swinging trot the fox gets about a dozen miles from his earth during the night, and, returning at daybreak, finds hounds between him and his strongholds. It is easy work outflanking them, but sooner or later a hum in the rear proclaims that some wanderer has struck his line. Half an hour's hard racing finds him exhausted— his night's work has already sapped his strength ; then on to the view sweeps the pack. A sharp race forward, a desperate snap at the foremost hound, a momentary check in the parti-coloured stream, a loud, rattling chorus, and bold Reynard's carcass lies still among the bracken.

The earths whence the red vermin make their journeys, it may be here remarked, might be whole districts from their extent. On Buckbarrow, for instance, standing at the heads of Kentmere, Mardale, and Longsleddale, the ground is tunnelled for the area of almost a square mile, one set of holes communicating with another.

The miles of passages generally baffle the 'cutest of terriers, and the great caverns have heard the death-shriek of many a fighting dog. If hunting is being carried on within the valleys mentioned, the escape of the fox has always to be prevented by blocking the chief entrances to this earth.

The following record of a day's hunt may show more clearly how the sport is carried on under the circumstances:

As I came round the corner of Kirkstone Fell from Woundale Moss, distinct sounds came from hounds from the side of Red Screes, and a few seconds later my eye was attracted by the huntsman's red coat crossing the skyline. The pack had therefore started three-quarters of an hour ago; but as there might be a delay before a huntable scent was discovered, I followed at my best pace. Fourteen hundred feet of grassy slack, crag, and scree had to be ascended, to the point where hounds had gone out of sight. In my eagerness, when threading the tortuous way among the crags, I made a wrong turn, leaving the grass benks for a more direct but steeper route. At one point I was climbing a rough ironstone gully, with screes shelving precipitously below, and succeeding this were loose stones. Twenty minutes after leaving the road, however, I passed the caërn on the summit. Windermere,

Coniston, Esthwaite, and Ullswater were all visible as I glanced around for the hounds. A faint bay came up the wind, then another; then straight over Scandale I detected figures moving among the boulders. They were, as the crow flies, about a mile and a half distant, but a deep valley lay between. I was not long in getting down the sixteen hundred feet into the dalehead, and then, for the first time, I saw a number of actively moving white dots among the crags. When within a quarter of a mile, the knot of men, who had not moved far during my approach, struck up the fell, leaving me struggling across the boulders at the foot of the crags. Gradually the yards separating us shrank down; then they turned round a crag-end and I lost view. The horn pealed again and again, and each time there was quite a chorus. Game was obviously afoot, and my first was likely to be my last glimpse of the hunting. In a few moments, however, a single hound came into view against the skyline; then I was standing among an inquisitive, sniffing crowd. The rousing signals which had so disconcerted me were those calling the pack from a hopeless scent. Four men followed, and we were heading leisurely back at a fair elevation above the dale, when one of the leading hounds gave the unmistakable triumphant 'find,' and the whole, dogs and men, rushed at top speed over very rough ground. Two hundred and fifty yards further on we recovered the pack around a storm-rent outcrop. Two terriers were slipped into the entrance to this 'hold,' and very shortly a series of fierce yaps and yells proclaimed that the tenant was giving fight. Bowman ordered hounds and followers to retire, hoping that the fox would make a dash into the open. Looking down a crack in the crags, our huntsman now espied Reynard, and asked us to help clear a passage. Accordingly, a good many pieces of rock were dislodged; but the venue of battle rapidly moving, our work was useless. At this time one of the terriers came out for fresh air, and was immediately seized. He had been at grips with Reynard. What a moan of delight that little draggled white creature gave as he was released! He instantly dashed into the dark opening and rejoined the fray.

As the minutes passed our force was augmented, till over a dozen men stood on the hillside. Bowman was desirous of digging the fox out, but there were no tools within miles. But wasn't the rock broken enough to be removed with pick and spade? In a short hour five or six tons of rock had been torn out, and a nine-foot-deep shaft sunk far towards the scene of conflict, where Jack and Nip had driven their fox to the extremity of its habitation. The wind was bitterly cold; on the bleak hillside there was no shelter from its pitiless sweep, and as afternoon wore on its current became charged with moisture. In the excavations matters were more lively than without. Eager, strong hands were passing out huge pieces of rock. The cliff had gradually been undermined some feet, and there was grave possibility of its splintered crest suddenly collapsing. After more tearing up of long narrow slabs of rock, a cavern was found, in which Bowman caught sight of one of his terriers; and he was kneeling over the tunnel, encouraging them, when a portion of the overhanging rock gave way. Every further effort was nullified by a shower of stones. Reluctantly the huntsman gave the word to come out, taking the terriers with us up the hillside. 'Give it a chance to come out;' but I detected in his voice that the fox was unlikely to do so. As a last resort, he picked up several boulders, and hurled them down the slope one after the other on to the roof of the fox's refuge. The first fragment bounced clear of the platform, but under its successor the top of the tunnel crashed in. At its next bound the rock struck the corner round which we had dug, and shattered it.

After another short wait we returned to our shaft, but found that another long toil was before us if we were to force the fox into the open. It was now quite certain that he would not do this till positively compelled.

'Let's hae t' terriers in agen, an' he'll happen stir.'

The splintering blow which had wrecked our work had apparently made no difference inside the earth, and Reynard was inaccessible as ever. There was nothing but to leave him in possession. But what had he suffered whilst our terriers beat him from pillar to post?

After this termination of the siege, the hounds went over the fell to Kirkstone, I following the valley to Ambleside, and so home. We had had four and a half hours' work among the rocks, but could not claim a kill.

Such a day of disappointment is occasionally inevitable, but the hunting more often suffers from the excess of events. When foxes returning from their night's prowl are converging on the main earths, it becomes a question, with so many afoot, which to follow first. The difficulty of keeping a pack together where scents are crossing here, there, and everywhere is very great. Often at the end of the day hounds are hunting in groups of four or five, each portion being followed by a section of 'the field.'

For hunting we prefer the spring to autumn, as

in the former period the ground is less liable to be sodden, and the mists are seldom so thick and persistent. Of course, deep snowdrifts are often lying in the northerly ghylls, and near these the going is heavy and unpleasant. We met at Sacgill, a picturesque cluster of old farmhouses at the head of Longsleddale. It was not yet daylight; stars glinted above in the clear, cold sky; a silvery crescent hung in the west; all round the dark hills sheered up skywards. Though the hour was so early, the people were up and doing the necessary day's duties by lantern light. As the first gray streaks of dawn rose in the east, the shepherd sallied out into the intakes to his flock, and the idlers adjourned to the temporary kennels. In a few minutes the door was opened and the hounds skeltered into the daylight, making the dalehead ring as the huntsman gave his preliminary wind of the horn. Then the shepherd came down the intake, and, as he got near enough, shouted that there was a big fox coming round the end of Dixon Crag—a mile and a half off as the crow flies. Having got so near home, it was more than likely that the redskin would risk all on his outpacing the hounds in the four miles to Buckbarrow. We toiled up a long ascent, near the top of which hounds struck a scent, and a wild crash of music proclaimed it red-hot. My old friend faced the slope no longer, but ran along it with a long, shambling stride.

'By gum!' he panted, when I got up to him, 't' ahld divvil 'll be in affor t' hooals er blockt' (the old devil will be in before the holes are blocked).

My attention had perforce to be confined to the ground we were crossing. It was like the débris of some huge cathedral piled block on block, and overgrown with parsley fern—so rough that in cooler moments I would have looked to avoid crossing it. A big ghyll furrowed the side of the fell, and away near the skyline the pack were pouring into it, and in a few moments climbing out on the further side. We had to cross the stream. The slope behind us made it difficult to leap, and the only hold beyond was on a slippery spur of rock. When we reached the hillside again the hounds were but a memory. Among dead bracken and across scree we ploughed determinedly, and in a few minutes reached a corner of the fell from which we caught a distant glimpse of the hounds in full cry. The huntsman was waiting here, and the whips. My companion, however, told me that the fox was now going to some 'stopped' holes, and would doubtless return quite close to hand.

After a seemingly interminable wait, a draggled fox, with back up, darted round a corner of the hill in front, and crossed the brook. A terrier was let loose. For a moment Reynard hesitated, then galloped forward; but the pugnacious animal was on him, worrying and snapping. The fox turned to his tormentor, but in a few seconds a loud chorus from the pack, which had been at fault, maybe, a moment, proclaimed the 'view.' The hounds seemed to shoot over every obstacle, and a turmoil of black-and-tan and liver-and-white, showed the death. The brush was rescued, but the head had been crushed out of all semblance by some iron jaw.

The next move was into a valley-head, where at every step a muddy fountain spurted over our boots from the spongy moss. From the east a dense white mist had been creeping over the mountains, completely hiding everything not close at hand. We heard, rather than saw, hounds pick up another trail, and soon the rousing calls of the hunt died away. The dalesmen with our party plodded along—tireless hunters they are—in the direction of the dying sounds. We were struggling along a rock-strewn gully, when the hounds again came faintly within hearing. There was an immediate rush across the craggy hillside; then the unmistakable sound pealed from below, its sharpness intensified by the mists around. At the foot of the rocky slope we ran into clear air, and saw the hounds lacing along an uneven grass plateau.

In a few minutes their quest apparently decided to take refuge on higher ground, so the pack again dashed out of view in the fog-banks. We had been moving in so many different directions that I had long since lost every sense of locality, and was forced to follow the others. The huntsman said the hounds would be found again when the mist blew up. The wind had been freshening all the morning, and was now hurling the unwieldy folds of mist forward; hill-tops rose boldly through the whirl, then were hidden as the next wave of cloud came along. Gradually, however, the veil dissipated, and the familiarity of the opening view struck me. When the last rag of vapour rolled from beneath, I saw Sacgill and the head of Longsleddale at our feet—we were standing near the grassy slope from which our hounds had chased their first fox. Again and again the huntsman sounded his horn; the hounds would make answer if they heard. Then we made back into Goat Scaur—a grand line of precipices near Buckbarrow—hoping to get a few together as we did so. The whip ultimately issued from a glen in Gray Crag as we came opposite. He had turned back with about half a dozen hounds after running a fox into an impregnable heap of boulders. In a while we heard another call—a trio of shepherds before whom five hounds had driven a fox round Branstree and into the Gatescarth, where they lost the scent. When a fair number of hounds and men had rallied, a visit was made to a benk where an old stager was in the habit of lying.

I had had enough of racing over sloppy grass and rough boulders, so stayed with another to watch for any stray hounds, which we were to take down the head to Sacgill. The horn echoed among the hills for awhile, gradually becoming fainter; then came a babel of distant sound and a speedy silence. Something that could run had turned up. In about an hour we had nearly a dozen hounds lying or sitting round us. ' It would be grand to have a hunt,' repeated my friend as he reviewed the dirty canines. ' Hark! holloa! ther's summat cummen across t' pass yed!' It was a fox, and apparently in a desperate hurry. ' Git t' dogs tagither.' The redskin was within five hundred yards before he became aware of any presence; then he pointed to go round us. ' He's followed, he's followed! Hurray! yon's Cumrade —Cu-um-ra-ade!' Our tiny pack had not yet seen the fox, but they were all excitement. Then Reynard, in diving down a slack, revealed his lean body, and hell for leather they pelted over grass and scree, through narrow ravines and over tiny cliffs, up, down, and across becks, we following for all we were worth. The fox was now over

the skyline, and we recovered our hounds as they
were getting on to the trail.   A bay from behind :
Comrade still had it, and he—the stoutest dog in
the pack—showed the way.   In a moment our dogs
were tearing along for very life or death.   Again
we put our best foot foremost, but became finally
at fault near a small waterfall.   The shepherd sat
down to eat the meagre lunch in his pocket, for,
said he, 'they'll not go far away, I'll warrant.'
After our meal we made to the nearest hill-top.
We reached the summit about two p.m., and
immediately my friend found a clue—we over-
looked a basin, in which was also a good deal
of crag and stony ground.   'Buckbarrow earth,'
said my companion ; 'and yonder's old Fishwick.'
I followed the direction, and saw a tiny column of
smoke rising from behind a crag.   Yes, Fishwick
had seen the hounds, and they were in Goat Scaur
now.   ' Jack, git ower to Nan Bield ; they'll come
that way oot.'

To Nan Bield was a good hour's walk, and we
stood near the caërn till the sun prepared to sink
behind Coniston Old Man.   The shepherd grew
impatient.   Perhaps the hounds had killed, or had
turned down the valley.   My friend was stamping
about among the snow to get a little warmth,
when he espied a fox moving over the hills towards
High Street.   'That beggar's black wet !   Whar's

t' hoonds?' In a few minutes we heard the hounds coming along, but on the wrong side of the hill. The shepherd cursed sonorously; our hounds had left the trail of the fox they had chased so far and bravely to respond to their huntsman's call, for he was also coming at a fair rate in the same direction. To tell how the new fox led us a dance round the head of Kentmere, how it paused on the very crest of High Street, and looked and longed for Swarthfell, then turned down the scree of Nanny Gap and made for Hill Bell, would be a long story. I shall ever remember that blind, blundering rush down the scree, when the loose débris rattled behind us. But the climax was reached soon after that. After negotiating some steep pieces of rock, the fox crossed the summit and dodged his followers. In a few seconds we saw him crossing a shoulder of the hill deep below. Down the scree dashed the hounds and one or two men whose blood was too hot for caution, and as we reached the bottom we found our fox had turned for the huge terraces of Rainsbarrow Crag.

His next move completely surprised us, for, instead of trying to get either above or below the cliffs, he took a line across the most dangerous portion. He had been viewed by the hounds, and they would follow to the end now. The

hounds, struggled across the head of a far-off
dale, and were lost to view again among the fells.
Whether old Cæsar escaped or died game will
never be known. If it were not for admiration
of his grim, relentless pursuers, we could wish
this plucky fox a longer life.

Collecting the pack after such a run would be
exceedingly difficult were it not that hounds,
when benighted, always make for the nearest
lights. Many a time the dales farmer is called
from bed in the small hours by the baying of a
stray hound outside his door. He may not
previously have been aware that hunting has been
afoot in his vicinity, but the animals, as long as
they are able, struggle down in full confidence of
a warm welcome.

Quite recently the Ullswater pack had a
tremendous run. During the day they routed
a fox out of a rocky ghyll on St. Sunday's Crag.
It immediately made over Fairfield, and, chased
hard, turned to Helvellyn. Here it temporarily
baffled the hounds, and turned again along the
side of the mountain to Fairfield. The pack were
now keeping it so actively employed that it could
not get to earth, and had to run over Red Screes,
passing the Kirkstone road near its summit.
There were only three hounds in the pursuit now,
and one of these but a young one. Away over

Kirkstone Fell and John Bell's Banner, across the rough Stony Cove and up High Street, the unattended chase went on. At the summit of the last-named fell the young hound had to confess defeat, but the other two kept up the pace, and finally killed their fox in Mardalehead. I am sorry that the exact mileage and total altitude cannot be established from the data to hand.

There is a very distinct element of danger in fox-hunting on the fells : a slip in crossing the screes at speed may mean a severe dislocation, and is almost certain to result in contusions of a more or less serious character, whilst a fall from any one of the crags crossed in a day's hunting is certain death. Many years ago a run was proceeding along the narrow ridge of Striding Edge just where it leaves the bulk of Helvellyn. Just as a particularly precipitous point was reached, one Dixon missed his footing and fell many yards. He was picked up quite dead. Still further into the past—about the middle of the eighteenth century—there occurred another accident, this time luckily not fatal. Hounds were slowly puzzling their way across the weatherworn face of Blea Water Crag in pursuit of a fox they had driven out of Mardalehead. By descending one or other of the steep ghylls, the more venturesome of the followers hoped to observe the hounds at work, and possibly head off the fox. Dixon (a common family name in the dales) essayed down a very crumbly watercourse, but lost his footing. Down he came with an awful smash, his body rolling and bounding down the rocks to a great depth, finally wedging itself into a corner of a ledge. Dixon never lost consciousness of his position, nor interest in the sport on hand, for, seeing the fox escaping out of a gully towards High Street, he called out to his comrades above :

' It's cummen oot be t' heigh end ! Lig t' dogs on, lads !' (It's coming out by the high end ! Lay the dogs on, lads !)

Often the hunt gets into risky places. A little while ago, at the break-up of a frost, there was a considerable rock-slip on Helm Crag, in the Grasmere Valley. Among the débris a fox made its home, and its depredations soon made it the terror of the countryside. When hounds next met in the valley, the huntsman was directed into the redskin's haunts, and a rare run ensued. Leaving the meadows, the scent lay up the intakes and into the screes beneath the great cliffs. It was soon apparent that hounds had no chance of overhauling the fox—he had had too long a start—but the hunt was pressed, in the hope that he might be turned out of home at length by a terrier. The pack finally stopped by a big heap of boulders, which it was difficult for a man to get near ; the recent slip had made the rock around so loose that at any moment hundreds of tons might hurl themselves down the hillside. Nothing deterred by the danger, the huntsman coolly scrambled into Reynard's fortress with his terrier. Small pieces of crag kept rolling down as the scree beneath was loosened by the approach of the man, and his position at length became untenable. Lancaster did not retreat, however, till quite sure that his terrier could not drive the fox from his tunnel home.

THE ANGLER IN THE LAKE COUNTRY

THE ANGLER IN THE LAKE COUNTRY

I. Trolling on Lake Windermere

An idler on the landing-stage pushed the rowlock with his foot ; the boat welted away a yard or two ; the right oar fended us from a maze of moored skiffs ; then, as arms and body swayed into rhythmic pendulations, we drew toward open water.

' Now, Jem,' said my companion to the walnut-bearded boatman, 'what's the likeliest bit for trolling ?'

' Millerground Bay for a start, then down the Belle Grange side awhile, and finish about t' Ferry.'

My intention in coming off this particular afternoon was to watch my companions' work. The angler was a big man, robust in muscle and rosy in face. The lake possessed few secrets from him ; with Jem at the oars, he had fished every shoal and round every islet and bay. Char and trout, pike and perch, on occasion provided him sport, and the worst of days was never wholly unfruitful. As an angler he might have faults : non-success was not now among them. Jem the boatman was a character in his way, and, chiefest interest to me, he was esteemed a first-class handler of a fishing-boat.

As the boat rattled through the wavelets I looked round. Maytime in Lakeland! Great boles and branches of thousands of forest trees almost hidden in a smother of green foliage, with here and there huge sprays of milk-white blossom where wild-cherry and crab-apple, whitethorn and blackthorn, grew. The fields between the wood-lands were tenderly and vividly green, while shadows of verdure climbed up the swelling mountain-slopes away on the horizon. This scene to the right : on our left and in front the waters of the lake sparkled, dotted with two or three islets green-crowned over a profusion of wild-flowers, and further away stood the dark fir-woods of Claife. We were now rapidly leaving the crowded bay, heading for where one or two boats slowly drifted.

'Those chaps are fishing with the fly,' said the angler. 'After all the rain yesterday, they'll do fairly well if they've plenty of time. But it's slow work with the fly with a bright sun like this; and yonder, in the shelter of the trees, there's hardly a ruffle on t' water.'

The afternoon was drawing to a glorious close ;

the sun had receded far. Quoth Jem, 'We'd better be starting,' as the boat approached within fifty yards of a little headland. At this the angler turned out a couple of rods, one for either side our craft. In a minute the lines were fixed. After allowing about forty feet he placed a switch, to which by lengths of gut were attached two spinners baited with perchlets. The angler drew my attention to the fact that trout find these little creatures more inviting when the strong pine-fin has been cut away. 'A perch in fighting trim is avoided by all sensible trout.' By this time Jem had the boat's head round, and we were facing a fair breeze from the south-west. The sun had plunged behind a heavy mass of cloud, and a shadow darkled across the water.

'Good!' chuckled the angler. 'Now, Jem, with a bit of luck we should do well.'

A dull, warm day with a fair ripple, I was given to understand, is ideal for the troller.

Immediately his lines had floated overboard the angler riveted his attention to the nodding rod-points. The oarsman continued to pull. He never made a splash sufficient to startle the shoals of fish in the depths beneath us. His strokes were just more than sufficient to counteract the drag of the ripples. Slowly, therefore, the boat crept on, its course nearly parallel with the shore.

My attention wandered as I looked over Calgarth's cylindrical chimneys to the groves of Troutbeck and the eternal fells. Jem, with eyes apparently shut, was plying his blades with stealthy touch and slight depths. The angler was intent on the lines trailing astern.

Then the angler moved at his vigil post astern. His practised hand was at the fastenings of the rod. The line jerked a little; then a portion of its length stretched taut and clear of the water—a bite at last. W—— was on his feet in a second, the rod freed in his hand. Jem ceased to row, and as the boat slowly drifted the contest between man and fish began. As the line slackened, W—— wound in warily, for he had felt that this was a big trout. The rod-top bent suddenly; his hand clapped a strain on the line. The trout was fighting steadily, and the long line was at first in his favour. At last I saw the top of a ripple ten feet away break, and a dark curling body came into view. Three seconds later an exhausted trout was squirming in the landing-net I held for its reception. A fine dark-coloured fish it was, too—one and a half pounds by the scale.

After this the boat was floated close inshore for half an hour without success till Jem rebelled, pointing out that we were nearly back at Bowness Bay. The boat was accordingly turned to cross

the lake.   As we glided along, lines towing astern,
W—— lit his pipe and began to talk.

'It was just in mid-lake here three years ago
that I caught a very big trout—over five pounds,
and strong and lively in proportion.   It was on
an evening such as this.   The char were here-
abouts that year, too.   You know, the char in
this lake keep in shoals, and move about altogether.   Just now they are in the upper basin.
They are gradually coming back to us.   But char-
fishing with the plumb-line is slow sport at best.
How is it done?   Well, like this : Imagine a
heavy sinker on a line from which hang by gut-
lengths as many as fifty hooks and baits.   That's
your tackle.   You row out to where the char are
lying, and drop your sinker overboard, taking care
that your baits don't foul one another in going
down.   Then you await results.   If your sinker
is too deep or not deep enough, you have your
time for nothing.   Hour after hour you sit trying
different depths and places, perhaps to find a
couple of small char caught at the end of a long
and trying day.'

At this moment a jerk at the nearer line
brought up this yarn abruptly.   There was a
lively bit of play as the trout doubled and dodged,
being backed and rushed in desperation, but finally
was played to the boatside completely drowned.

The other line was also taken at the same time, but this was only a nibble.

'I like perch-fishing best,' said Jem, as he leant on his oars. The last down-steamer was passing, churning the waters into foam and creating a strong water. 'Do you remember, Mr. W——, that droppy June day under the trees at Miller-ground? We were out but four hours for over two hundred fish. But, then, bass aren't worth much, so we were hardly into pocket.'

This phenomenal catch, I need hardly mention, was due to my friends coming across a large school of perch suddenly taken with 'biting mania.' At such time anything is risen at, and the sport only concludes when the last member of the school is captured. I have watched in clear water a perch taken struggling wildly from between companions, each of which, undeterred, took the same bait within a minute.

'Do you have much trouble with pike?' I asked, anxious to get their opinions on each of the important denizens of the lake.

'Well, no; pike are fairly kept down by using trimmers, and the Angling Association nets when-ever it is possible. There's not half so many pike as there used to be.'

'There's a story that when Professor Wilson was once rowing near the Ferry he picked up a couple of exhausted pike. They were of almost equal size, and one had tried to swallow the other head first, with the result that the head had fixed in its throat, choking it.'

'Oh yes,' responded Jem, 'I have talked with one of the men who picked up the two fish. But it's nothing fresh for two pike to try that game on. I have seen them myself chewing halfway up one another's bodies. Pike cannot loose their jaws after they have once gripped a thing. I got a pike at Wray once with its teeth still fixed in the body of a two-pound trout.'

By this time we were progressing in the shade of the fir-woods. It was grand to hear the breeze whisper just above, and here and there came the rattle of a rivulet down the rocky bluffs. For an hour Jem rowed and paused alternately. A goodly haul of fish was present in the well of the boat at the finish.

With my face over the side of the boat, I looked down into deep, still water, and, though it was evening, the bottom, scarred with rocks and tiny cliffs, was in full view. In my idlings I conjured up from this flat boulder the image of a boat; from that muddied pile of fragments the semblance of a ruined cottage; here a patch of stoneless lake-bed stood for a field, with rugged heaps of rock for boundaries. But as daylight faded away the subaqueous panorama failed me. The sky above the fir-trees glowed with crimson and orange; the zenith was bright blue flecked with white cloud-wrack. Then, to the sound of cracking whips and hoarse voices, to the regular hoofings of horses and the discordant groanings and shriekings of braked wheels, the wood-waggon made its difficult, dangerous way down a dell to the narrow by-road. And further away up the slope the sound of the woodman's axe died away as semi-darkness told him that the long day's task was over.

We had now been afloat over four hours, so that a meal was due to us. Jem turned over his coat which had laid in the stern, and produced a large packet from his pocket. W—— had provided a basket of food, fortunately, so we fell to. I might have said that the meal was washed down by draughts of clear water from the lake, but the element upbearing our craft tasted — how shall I say it? — insipid, tasteless, or, perhaps more accurately, rather flat. After a short interval my companions produced tobacco and pipes, and a thick fragrance hung in the air. W—— took up his strain of tutor again.

'In trolling, the chief things to bear in mind are soundless rowing, baits on a long line, face the wind if possible. A breeze, take it for granted, will never blow you exactly along the line you wish to follow. As to where to fish, round islets and near shoals are the best places, while about thirty yards from shore, where the lake-bed suddenly falls away to a great depth, is a very safe place for fish.'

The pipes were puffed pensively awhile after this ; then Jem the lustful spoke out :

'What a night this would be for lathing ! In my father's time this boat, instead of hauling four baits through the water, would have had a hundred or more. Laths, each with six hooks, would have been dotting the water thirty yards either side of us, and a boat-load of fish would have been landed.'

Without laths, however, our sport had been deadly enough, and at last, while the night was still young, the lines were finally hauled in, and through steely darkness we glided up the narrow sleeve of water between Curwen's Isle and the mainland to Bowness and to bed.

II. Out with the Bracken-clock

During the hot, close days of June there is but one lure which invariably succeeds when angling in mountain waters, and that is the bracken-clock—a beetle somewhere about half an inch in length, possessing tiny wings and sheathed in tough scales, which then swarms along the hillsides.

We were assured of an ideal day for tarn-fishing when we left our quarters, and had agreed to stick to the uptrending path till the tarnside was reached. But our resolution went for nothing, as we turned to the moorland beck at the first opportunity. Though tempered somewhat by the breeze, the sun's power was unpleasantly in evidence. No tree was there in the whole upland valley large enough to render us shade, and the companionship of the rattling brooklet seemed to render our walk cooler and more tolerable. The infant Lowther was as usual crowded with tiny fish; the few large ones seen here and there among the smaller fry had apparently run up from the adjacent lake. To these we would have liked to have paid attention, but in general the water ran so low and clear that succcess seemed impossible.

One thing about Mardalehead strikes me as peculiar : you look up the dale from the hotel or from the side of Branstree, and it seems as though the descending rivulets are like continuous threads dancing in the sunshine ; but only when you begin to follow the brooks closely do you find what cunning little dubs and gullies are hidden away among the rolling hillocks. I knew that one of these concealed reaches held a deep pool in which were several large trout. Coming down from a climb of High Street, the steep front-face of which glowers into Mardalehead, two evenings ago I had lain by the rock-dub and watched the rising trout. They were then taking some small insects which the current was washing down.

This morning I approached cautiously. The sun was shining straight into the narrow gorge, lighting up the veil of spray from the spouting fosse with brilliant rainbow hues. The bracken fronds, almost dipping into the waters, were swarming with winged life, the glossy clocks being most abundant. The then sandy soil also teemed with red ants, while caterpillars of many sizes hung on the stems of the heather.

'What shall I put on?' queried my companion, as he picked up for closer examination a particularly fine clock.

'That, of course,' I replied; 'and drive your hook well home, for they are tough customers, and will wriggle off if you don't mind. The trout here won't look at a bare hook.'

J—— got himself into a good position, and after a few attempts dropped his line where the fish were lying. The distance was short, but the rock-basin was small and fringed with branches of holly, alder, and rowan. It was apparent that the trout were going off the feed, for the sun was becoming more and more powerful, but two or three were not yet gorged. At J——'s fourth throw, directed towards the bubbles and ripples around the fall, a fine yellow trout floated up to and annexed the beetle. I was waiting my turn to cast—for two lines could not be plied at once in such narrow quarters—so saw the whole struggle. J——'s line jerked taut, bringing the surprised fish almost to the surface; then it doubled back towards the foot of the pool, going deeper as the slackened line allowed it, till when my friend at last checked it; his line was almost fouled among the heather twigs. There was a fine piece of play here—through the transparent water every evolution of the fish was clear to me—but in a few minutes the trout

tired and came within the swoop of J——'s landing-net.

Fishing on unsuccessfully for some half-hour,
we had decided that the next would be our last
cast, when a lethargic trout to which I had already
dangled clock and ant was aroused to indiscretion
by the appearance of a fat green caterpillar on the
top of the whirlpool, apparently just tumbled from
the swaying rowans above. In a flash the floating
morsel was sucked in, and the hidden barb struck
home. So surprised was the trout at this inter-
ruption of his day-dream that I had him clear of
the whirlpools and almost on to the narrow shingle
at my feet before he began to struggle. It was a
splendid example of the brown trout, but I was
disappointed at its tame, tardy fight for freedom.
We spent, encouraged by this success, another half-
hour by this force, but no further reward being
forthcoming, we decided to make a move towards
the mountain tarn.

Over the lowering crags we could see huge
masses of vapour gathering in north and west, and,
as our local oracle promised, these clouds spread
so widely that by noon the sun's rays were shorn
of most of their radiance. The air, however,
became close almost as the puff from a mammoth
oven, and this though the breeze was at this
elevation powerful enough to make a tidy ripple

on the tarn's surface. Walking along the shore by the outlet, I now observed a common tragedy of to-day in Nature. There was a whirring of minute wings, and close to my ear there passed the usual bracken-clock. It was wafted by the wind some twenty yards over the water before its weak wings refused to uphold its carcase longer, and down with a faint thud the insect dropped.

The breeze blowing right across the tarn carried it struggling along for a short way ; then there was a glimpse of a curved fin above the water, an extra dimple in the ripples, and the insect had been taken down by some voracious trout or perch. In a few seconds I had another clock on my line and swung it out to near where the previous one had disappeared. The hook had hardly reached the water before I felt the jerk of a ' bite.' There is no fine nibbling by the trout where the clock is concerned, and therefore almost anyone can strike successfully. The fish I had on was a lively customer, and more than once I feared an escape, but the hook was too deep to be wrenched out by error of judgment. When at last it came into the shallows and was netted, I had time to consider. My friend further up the tarnside was some time in achieving a capture : he was casting too short by far. In a mountain tarn such as this it is necessary that the fly or bait be cast as far out as possible. The water goes very gradually deeper for some twenty yards from the shore, then falls away to great depths almost precipitously.

Just beyond the point where the deep and shallow so nearly meet the chief shoals of fish usually lie. In flood-time, and of nights in summer, they approach the beck mouths for food, and may be here taken; but during the day the most successful angler is the one who can throw most accurately to a great distance. To-day there was little difficulty in seeing where the fish lay; constantly they dashed at the floating carcases, frequently a double rise occurring when two selected the same morsel. We angled on for a while, hardly moving from our first selected stations, and meeting with fair success, till we felt it high time for something to eat. At our *al-fresco* luncheon we turned out our panniers and compared their contents. Though the water is without preservation, and its outgoing rivulet impassable for trout, this tarn had for years offered to anglers a fair stock of fish, averaging three to the pound. In the twenty lying on the shingle more than half were half-pounders. No other tarn in the same basin could give a return equal to this, though many are closely watched and their stock frequently replenished. Moreover — and this peculiarity was uniform to a marked degree — every fish was covered with large crimson blotches, more than treble the normal size.

After our meal we returned to the waterside ; the dimples caused by rising fish became fewer and fewer, and our sport waned. By about four p.m. the shoals within casting range were unapproachable, though now and again there would be a sharp sequence of rises further out. Had I not flogged and played myself tired by this time, I doubt not that the curious poaching instrument I had picked up from beneath a boulder would have found employment. The lath, as used on our mountain tarns, is a short board, its lower edge weighted so as to float the whole upright, to which are attached several baits on short lengths of gut. The contrivance is floated out from some point where the breeze can cause it to move, and allowed to cross the most fishy portions of the water. Of course, the operator need give it little attention in transit. He retrieves it on the further shore, and easily lands what trout there are on the hooks. The method is a most deadly one, and I am glad that there was no real temptation to resort to it.

III. AT MAYFLY TIME

ABOUT the period when the angler in mountain tarns
watches for the bracken-clock, his confrère by less
elevated waters is eagerly looking for the coming
of the mayfly. In pools set like diamonds in
green woods, or in the still reaches of streams,
night fishing is now much resorted to. The
gauzy-winged mayfly flutters about as long as a
glimmer of light plays on the face of the waters,
while long after amber night has settled over field
and wood and height the trout remain on the feed.

It is evening. A narrow road carries us rapidly
towards fresher and cooler air. The luscious
green of unshorn fields, decked with starlike
forms of white and red and blue, is giving place
to the domain of bramble and gorse and rock
scarce veiled with soil. At the summit of the
road the glories of sunset burst upon us. The
sun is sinking between a thin cloud and a line of
rugged hill-tops. Through this interval rays of
silver and red and pearl are gleaming, dividing the
blue west as though with ploughshares of heaven's

own fashioning. But to us chiefest interest lies in the gleaming waters in the middle distance. A fir-wood bounds their further shore ; gorse and whin grows luxuriantly on the moor around. One or two small islets, hung with lichen-poisoned sallows, are in the larger section ; the merelet is almost divided by two jutting tongues of scrub.

In ten minutes we are by the water's edge. The gorgeous lights in the western sky have dulled ; rose succeeds the fiery red, silver turns to yellow and to gray-blue. The air resounds to the wingings of tiny insects, yet there is a great peace underneath it all. Broken—yes, broken by the quavering wail of the plover pacing the grassy marge near its nest ; by an occasional crash, as a heavy trout leaps high and falls back from its keen pursuit. But stay a moment yet, ere the rod is drawn out, to watch the ephemeræ dancing just above the surface of the water. They wheel in scores, they soar by hundreds ; yet every movement seems to bring death close, for one here and one there, in a clumsy swerve, touches the water : its frail wings are damped so that it cannot rise again to the airy quadrille of its companions. But they mark not its absence. The dangerous game is not checked. The fallen insect makes one or two attempts to raise itself ; in wild, erratic circles it spins round and round, is floated by the faint breeze of eventide toward the shore at our feet. Yard after yard it gradually comes nearer; then suddenly we see the triangular back-fin of a trout in close attendance. A flash—the fin has disappeared; another, and the dark body of a trout leaps half out the water, and as it supplely curves over the poor mayfly is forced into a maw already distended with like unfortunates.

Scores of fish are on the alert to-night—'the water is fair wick wi' 'em,' as our companion says —waiting for the downfall of the aerial rejoicers just out of their reach, though here and there an impatient one makes a huge leap for a bonne-bouche.

In a trice the rods are out and ready; every moment is of value, for tarn trout are capricious in their feeding periods, and may suddenly and absolutely cease to rise to their most cherished atoms. J—— takes left and I take right shore and begin. I am hampered at first by a series of tiny bogs, but in a few yards reach a gorse-covered promontory. This proves a capital station for a cast; my line swings far and true to where I last saw a struggling mayfly sucked down. My fly— why, a moment ago I picked up and impaled a mayfly, far less difficult to manage than the armour-plated bracken-clock. In less than five minutes my first trout was ashore, a monster over two pounds in weight. But this is a mere of great trout. I remember some six years ago the bed, which had been drained for some time, being reflooded, and a large number of yearling trout being turned in. For some seasons no angling was done. The stock grew great in size, though doubtless, seeing there are no redds, not even a streamlet passable for minnows, available, there was no increase in numbers. The feed is abundant, weeds and other cover plentiful, and, save for the cursory (and cursed) visits of a swan from a mill-dam some miles away, the enemies to fish-life are few.

While these observations are being passed, my rod is being plied assiduously. My fly, planted though it often is in tempting positions over lurking trout, is again and again drawn out untaken. A sharp eye has my quest. See! the wings of the fly, though as deftly placed on the water as my craft finds possible, are bedraggled with constant immersion, and is therefore considered unpalatable by the fish. It doesn't take a moment to change it, and with the next cast—aimed at that monster in the lee of that islet, behind whose descending shoulders the parted waters have just gurgled together—comes success. The faint feel of a bite travels to my hand, and I strike. There is a sudden slack of the line ; then, as the rod-point is raised to continue

the strain, a dead pull; then to right the trout
makes a sudden rush. I scarcely have followed it
than forward my fish dives and downward, and to
the resistance is added the entanglement of a bunch
of water-weeds. Carefully I get my trout away from
this. There is another run forward—a more dis-
turbing one this time indeed—followed by a cl'ck
backward and a salmon-like leap a yard out of the
water. I am taken aback at the manœuvre, and
Salmo levenensis has obtained some valuable yards
of liberty, each adding to its chances of breaking
away; and, sure enough, with what must have
been a double back-turn by the fish, my line is
hitched round a hidden snag, and, as my trout and
I put on pressure from our opposite ends, parts.

What size did it look like as that leap was
made? Nay, trouble me not. The rascal has
got a hook and a piece of gut, undeniably my
property, and is still at large, if a trifle discom-
moded. Well, well! J—— had a turn with a
cunning trout from this point three evenings ago,
and was defeated more ignominiously even than
I; so *he* can't crow over me. But that fish
knows its way about in a fashion and practises
manœuvres I for one don't like.

My next trout, obtained after hooking a submerged tree and tangling in a clump of water-
lilies, fights gamely and gives me some breathless

moments. When it comes to the landing-net, I am surprised at its smallness, considering its splendid defence—four ounces or less. Well, back it goes! It deserves a new lease of freedom.

Now the gorging trout retire to the middle of the tarn. It is provoking to watch them rising freely far out of reach. Then the silence deepens; the sharp splashes and gurgles of rising trout gradually stop. My rod must be laid aside, for J—— is signalling across the water.

'Come on round!' he calls. 'I want some baccy.'

If J—— is not fishing, he must be smoking; therefore he is perpetually running short of some adjunct to his passion. We will walk quietly round to where he is.

From the reed-beds the coot murmurs to its mate; now and again we hear soft rumblings as they paddle about. A bevy of wild-duck squabble in undertones at another point. J—— has wandered up the further shore meanwhile. A plover whirls up from his feet, 'squealing like a stuck pig.' He growls as we fiercely denounce his carelessness.

The soft cutterings in the reed-beds cease as the wild 'teeu-wits' re-echo over the tarn; worse than that, in the half-light we see a small dark body nimbly run along, and without a splash take the water. It is an otter disturbed from his nightly gleaning of crayfish. Now we come to the head of the tarn. A wide series of bogs and mud-holes, with a straggly path over the few sound spits of grass, lie in front of us. We can see the distant hills limned against the softly starlit sky. Bay and shore and bush on either side the faint blue water are in fair sight; but though the fairies have traced it with tufts of bog-cotton, the narrow track is invisible to us. One or two slight slips, ankle-deep in a slough, and we are halfway across. Here a stretch of water, perhaps eight feet wide and a foot deep, interposes—the channel by which on occasion storm-water drains from the upper bogs. Many a slab of rock has been placed here to expedite the crossing, but in a week each has sunk too deep in the soft ooze to be of use. To find the uppermost of the stones to-night will require nicety of judgment, even though the landmarks before and behind us are easily recognisable.

'Nothing venture, nothing have.' A frolicsome youth essayed to cross here in broad daylight not many moons ago. He made two steps safely, then trod on the edge of a stone, which capsized and threw him into the channel. He was fished out covered with mud and slime. However, to-night we encounter no such tragedy.

J—— now calls on us to hurry up. We crash through the prickly gorse to his side.

'Do you know, you fellows, what I have just seen? A moment ago a big eel—I could see it clearly in the dark—slid down that grass-track and took the water. It must have come down from the other tarn'—a quarter of a mile away.

'Old Jack Brock tells of meeting an eel sliding one wet night between Skeggleswater and Longsleddale. It was more than half a mile from a stream big enough for it to swim in.'

'Bedad!' interposes J——, whose knowledge of natural history is full of strange intervals of ignorance, 'and do eels swim? I thought they wriggled along the bottom like snakes.'

These episodes of eel-travelling may be a little beyond the truth, but J—— doesn't believe so, giving as evidence against our sweeping assertions to the contrary some marvellous fish-lore. After that he clutches the tobacco-pouch closely, and in a few minutes a reek of pungent smoke tells us that his passion demands whole-hearted attention.

The trout come on the feed again ere morning. They are specially eager by the shallows, where hundreds of becalmed mayfly corpses await them. J—— avers at dawn that he saw a trout rub itself against a reed on which a mayfly hung with such violence that the insect was dislodged, fell into the water, and was eaten up.

IV. Evening Fishing

One of our best beats lies between the mill-sluice and the top of Beckmickleden. The long shallow dam is succeeded by pools to the old ford, above which is a rocky stretch, and then more pools, some floored with mud and shingle, others with naked rock. Coppices fringe one side of the stream the whole way, and the lavish falls from their overhanging branches go some way towards attracting large fish to these haunts. At flood-time few anglers are disappointed of heavy panniers, but the chief repute of the water is for evening fishing. Many a time alone or with a companion have we wandered along this portion of the river.

The day had been hot and bright; but at evening a faint breeze stirred the leaves, and around the declining orb the clouds formed into a solid bank. I now saw my friend approaching along the riverside, rod in hand. This lean, alert man was one of the best fly-makers and selectors for miles around, and the river held no secret from him. Where everyone else failed he succeeded. He knew where the best fish lay, and the surest methods to get them. Our greetings were short, for I required little urging to join in an expedition to the upper waters.

In ten minutes we approached a water-hewn ravine, and shortly reached the upper mill-dam. Across the narrow stretch of wimpling dark waters, buried almost by towering elms, was a tiny hamlet, but on our side a cornfield was fronted with a row of bloom-spangled briar-roses. The station selected was near the foot of the pool, a place from which we could throw to the vicinity of the sluice. My companion chose me a couple of winged flies, and told me to cast lightly, as the water was bringing down a good many dead insects from the grasses and trailing bushes in its course. Rod in hand, I stood a moment. The fish were rising a long way out, and it took time to get the flies so far without a splash. I had been conceded the best situation, and my friend had gone some way upstream, where he had located fair sport. It would, perhaps, be five minutes before I got my line into the right place, but when I did success came fairly promptly. I was ruefully considering how long my spine and shoulders would stand the labour, when my fly was sucked down. I struck, but without success. Sir Trout had selected a floating body not six inches from where my counterfeit floated. In the second I had looked round for my companion, my eye had been off the lure, and it speaks well for the flymaker's skill that I could not distinguish my own among the others floating down. I was raising my rod to try another cast, when the fly was taken in reality—not leapt at with a sudden splash, but quietly sucked down without its taker raising a ripple. I could scarce believe it had gone, till a faint tremor passed up the distended line, and then I struck home. Instantly I knew that a big trout was on tow, for my rod swayed and bent as I put on strain. The fish did its little best to get off, but wrist and eye worked for once in unison, and I speedily was reeling it along the surface. This proved to be a dark-coloured trout, but the next was a beautifully scaled one— my friend pronounced it a *Salmo iridens*, the American rainbow trout, a number of which had some time since been turned into the river.

The head of this dam has deteriorated from an angler's point of view since a family of swans were quartered on it. In my school-days old Jimmy, our veteran angler, would frequently stand by the mouth of the marsh drain there, and take his six or eight fish regularly every evening for a week.

A few minutes on, casting at every rise in the purling dubs, and following down every whirlpool, we come to the old ford, and then the bridge. To-night the occupants of the deep pool are not inclined to feed.

Above the bridge the river descends for about two hundred yards over very rocky bottom, where the stream swirls down without a pool or a yard of slack water. During the last two years a fringe of wych-elm has been rooted out on this side, and a number of good casting-places opened up, for under cover of frothing waters good fish frequently lie, and there is great exhilaration in fighting a stout trout on whose side is the stream commanding a heavy drag on both line and prize. Immediately we reached this point T—— came up with a fresh fly, a gray drake. This fly is not very popular with local anglers, but my friend explained that, after several seasons of close observation, he had found no fly of equal merit during close, warm evenings on this reach of rushing water. I had been previously referred to another local enthusiast for corroboration. 'Yes,' said he, in a quaint, homely dialect impossible to transfer to paper, 'one night we were coming down by the Low Barn, and Tom told me of the gray drake. I didn't believe in it, so he put one on for me. The water was dashing down and splashing among the stones, but after a bit I found a fish. And, sure enough, at the drake it came with a rush. Well, I threw again and again at different places, getting in ten minutes three of the finest fish I ever did. Then my luck seemed to change, and though I got plenty of bites I could never land a fish. Tom at last got disgusted with my bad work, and prepared to take the rod over, but on examining the fly we found that the hook had broken off short at the shank. Of course, my failures were thus explained with honour.' Our own experience at this point was much as above ; I will not inflict details.

By this time the evening waxed old, the sky grew dusky, the fiery red in the west faded to rose colour, then died out to a faint blue, which as the hours passed intensified to azure, to indigo, and to ultramarine. In the north a pale sheen lit up the sky almost to the zenith—the night-glow—and here by the riverside, between the partly-light sky and the mirroring waters, there was no difficulty in making out any necessary detail. The black gnat had disappeared about sundown, but my friend was now using large sulphur-coloured moths. As in coming up we had used three different lures, I asked if any further variation would be necessary, but the bustard would hold till daybreak, when the hour for clear water worm arrived. Personally, in fishing this reach I should have held to black gnat and night-owl only.

On one side of the long pool selected for our evening's angling the land rose in a sheer oak-clad bluff, while on the other the coppices, interspersed with flowery avenues, swelled upward in less abrupt line. The fishing was delightful; over the mellow rattle of the incoming stream now and again came the splash as a trout leapt up at the flies whirling above. Our station was in the shadow, else our movements would have been clear to the fish. My friend told me a true angler's story concerning this dub. After an evening's angling, he and another were sitting on a rock smoking and talking in subdued tones. Suddenly there was a scuffle almost beneath their feet, and Jack struck towards the scene of the disturbance with his rod-stock. There was a sudden squeal, and the surprised anglers found that the random blow had almost decapitated a young rabbit. Doubtless, frisking along as is common with its kind, it had not noticed the angler's proximity. After an hour's successful work we moved still further upstream, clear of the ravine. Here the river has worn a narrow channel into the upper edge of a rock-stream, forming a deep pool, in which iris and long aquatic grasses flourish. The light here was much better, and I rapidly reduced my experienced companion's lead in captures. At about one a.m. there was a short pause in the fish's feeding, during which we cast in vain. My comrade promptly noticed this, and for half an hour we left the waterside that he might show me the hole in the ground where some two hundred dead swallows were found after a late sudden frost, and also to take me to a circle of ancient dwarf crab-apple trees, planted, he averred, by Druids of old. In this expedition we also came across a heron, standing poised on one leg in shallow water. Scared at our approach, it winged away uttering a wild alarum; and we were surprised to notice three others of its gaunt kindred make away from near reaches. Of other waterside life, the otter since dusk had been frequently in sight—he lives without fear of a pack nowadays in our river ; the dipper and the kingfisher had retired at sunset, but the whitethroat's song had been constantly in our ears. Game, unseen, had rustled hither and thither in the coverts.

The sky to eastward was brightening when we returned to our rods. My companion told me to do my best, for time was passing ; but never a bite came my way. He was more fortunate, for a long cast down the dub was taken. The fish on feeling the barb, however, went through a number of desperate manœuvres. I heard the struggle, then noticed my friend disgustedly drawing in his line. Probably by tangling the gut round some jagged corner of rock the fish had got away.

V. About the Fish-spear

Every hour of the short period the salmon spends in fresh water his life is threatened. The sportsman's method is by rod and line, but the poacher kind incline to the net and the fish-spear. The use of the former has been frequently and fully described; but the spear, not being favoured by the wholesale plunderers of our streams, has been less to the fore. The fish-spear, gaff, or leister (practically, if not quite, identical weapons), is used by the occasional poacher mostly, by the labourer who cannot resist the temptation to take one or two of the great salmon occupying the rock-pools in his immediate vicinity.

There was at one time a practice, in the Derwent and other salmon streams of our Lake Country, of spearing the fish from horseback. The horse was driven into mid-stream at some shallow where the uprunning fish were bound to show themselves, and the rider, armed with a long lance, struck at such fish as he could reach. Apparently some of our forefathers were very keen on this sport, for over a hundred years ago a certain gentleman offered a public wager to kill more salmon from horseback in a stated stream than any comer. So far as records show, the challenge was never taken up. Clarke, the pioneer of Lake Country angling literature, states that in his day (*circa* 1760) many gentlemen came regularly to Patterdale in autumn to join in the sport of spearing the great lake trout which had run up the Goldrill from Ullswater.

Dalesmen carried torches at night to the great pools to show the sportsmen where the shoals of spawning fish lay. The result of this wholesale destruction was that the monster in question—its weight is variously estimated from sixteen to sixty pounds and over—gradually dwindled in numbers, and is now almost, if not quite, extinct in the great lakes.

My earliest recollection of the leister is also my earliest of anything pertaining to angling. Below our two-arch stone bridge is a pool, perhaps twenty yards long and fifteen wide. During great floods in autumn, salmon very occasionally pass the weirs as far as this, beyond which they are never seen. There was some little excitement, therefore, when the blacksmith showed a salmon resting in the bridge-dub, and at once attempts

were made to capture it. But the fish frequented
the rushing waters just behind the cut-water of
the bridge, and no one could get at it. A neighbouring farmer brought his gun, and fired three
shots without effect. I fancy, as I recall the
creamy turmoil at that point, his mark would be
a difficult one. Finally the blacksmith forged a
fearful weapon—a hand garden-fork fixed on to
a shaft. Armed thus, he clambered down the
cut-water as near as possible to his quarry, and
made several lunges. I remember well, for I was
not far away, leaning over the ledge of the bridge,
seeing the square tail of the fish show through the
froth of the 'rush' as it turned downstream.
But though this attempt was a failure, the smith
and the cobbler and the villagers assembled noted
that, when disturbed from its favourite haunt, the
giant retired to the shade of a big tree just below.
With this extra information, the smith climbed
down next day to where the fish was lying, and,
carefully poising his weapon, I watched him
plunge it again and again at an invisible body in
the water. Then up he scrambled at great pace,
crossed the bridge out of my sight, and disappeared down the stile at the other end. I heard
a crackling of boughs, and a few moments later
Dove returned carrying the big fish—I remember
that its tail was flapping convulsively—in his

leathern apron. Of course, the whole affair was kept as quiet as possible, lest the water-bailiff, hearing, should bring the law down on the offenders. Being a very small child, my presence was unheeded; but, try as they would, the cobbler and the smith could not persuade me that the heavy burden in the leathern apron was simply a black river-cobble. I insisted it was the fish. Years later I was told that my recollection of the whole affair was quite correct.

The favourite period for spearing the fish is, of course, during the hours of darkness. More than once I have seen men rendezvous in a lonely spot near our weir. Many a salmon getting thus far up the river at nightfall lies in the deep rock-basins till day returns, and on that his enemies reckon. In the woods fringing the rocks, a close search will at any time discover three or four leisters hidden by their most recent users. As dusk deepens into night the poachers come out; only one is armed with a spear, the other carrying a bag, and the third a dark lantern. When the water's edge is reached, a brief ray shows where the fish are lying. The spearman, picking out his fish, plunges his weapon. If the stroke goes true, the salmon is rapidly jerked out, to be killed by the bagman. This goes on so long as a fish can be reached.

At other times, from the windows of a rural lodging, I have watched just before dawn stealthy lights flickering by the pools in another river, and two or three hours later have breakfasted off salmon showing leister-marks. Leistering being, of course, a slow process, the villagers alone are supplied, but at a rate per pound which seems to make the game very unsatisfactory from a profit point of view.

I have in my mind's eye one particular scene. In half-flood the river is dashing beneath a hog-backed stone bridge; all around is darkness. The lower slopes of the great braes are invisible, their summits but dimly in view against the cloudy sky. Now and again a few stars rush across a rift in the upper blackness. Along the water a dim, uncertain light plays, showing sharp currents breaking and swirling over unseen reefs, or roaring in white fury against the dark, un-yielding boulders here and there visible in the bed. After a few minutes' wait, a labourer comes panting up; he is a well-known 'small-scale' poacher, the plague of the keepers for miles around.

'Old Carson is out to-night,' said the new-comer, 'but he's away up behind the weir.'

For a moment we didn't gather the meaning of this, nor of the immoderate fit of laughter our acquaintance indulged in. Then it struck us that, by making a long détour, he had wiled the water-bailiff far from the series of pools we intended to 'work.' In a moment we were over the wall and were deep among the ash-woods fringing the water, following the poacher, who trod the narrow, stony path with the ease and silence of long accustom. In a few minutes he stopped. So intense was the shadow that we cannoned into him before we knew of his halting.

'Mind where you are coming,' he growled, in a whisper. As he spoke we could hear a faint dragging and a rustling of dead leaves somewhere in the darkness near his feet. Now we came into the river-bed, where it was comparatively light. The poacher, we saw, had drawn a leister, as well as a bag and a lantern, from a secret place in the river-bank. In a few seconds he prepared for action ; then, handing me the lantern, he spoke in a low voice :

'You keep close to me, and when I give the word turn the light on to the slack water. And you '—turning to my companion—'had better pick up and bag what fish I stick [pierce].'

Now the three of us crawled stealthily along the rocks bounding the rushing stream. Slack water indeed! In that tumult of fosse and rock and rapid it did not seem likely that a yard of smooth surface would be found. But my judgment was wholly amiss. Here and there, between the eddying current and the hard shore, were quite long stretches without a single ripple, and near the head of one such the poacher stopped suddenly.

'There'll be something here,' he said. At a rustle of his hand I glided forward. 'Now show a light on the water just in under my feet.' I did so, and there quite half a dozen silver-sided salmon lay, with their heads upstream, never thinking that that vagrant gleam meant death for one or more of their number. I saw the spear plunge into the water; the nearest fish turned, struck through the vitals, floating in the faint swirl towards the head of the pool. My companion, however, was alert, and seized the carcass before it was tumbled far away down the stream. Meanwhile the poacher prepared for another stroke; again I directed my shaft of light, and again he struck. But the shoal had floated further into the stream, and he failed to reach them from that station.

Now he stepped waist-deep into the pool, directing me to move so as to give a very brief flash *across* the water. I did so, and another kill was registered, after which the poacher proposed that we should try another place. Accordingly, we moved downstream, walking wherever possible in the shadow of the trees.

A great trough between high banks was our next halting-place. Looking carefully through a screen of bushes, we saw dim figures moving about the lower end of the level water.

'Some poachers from the town, I reckon,' whispered our spearman. 'They're fools to try netting here, where there's hundreds of rocks on the bottom to tear their net to ribbons.' Half an hour or more we stood there watching with all our eyes. But little did we gather, save that the poachers were not averse to plunging into the ice-cold stream to release their net whenever fouled by a boulder or a piece of sunken brush-wood. Then, 'Lie down, quick,' whispered frantically the poacher; and though we were standing on a bed of soaking, half-rotten leaves, down we went. On the moment, up into the sky from a point just beyond the far end of the pool, soared a rocket. My eyes watched its flight anxiously, watched it burst into a shower of stars which, slowly floating down, illuminated wood and water and rock clearly. The keepers evidently had knowledge of some trespassers. Was it of us or of the netmen, who at the first roar of the rocket dispersed into the woods, abandoning their net in the river? The poacher's sharp eyes had seen the first spark struck by the keepers, and he had warned us as far as possible.

We were clearly in a predicament. Run for it! No ; long ago every avenue from the woods would be guarded. With the wet soaking through our clothes, we lay in the thicket. One of the netmen rushed past, crashing through the dead branches within a yard of us. Half a minute later there was a shout and the sounds of a scuffle from the direction he had taken. Another minute, and, horridly suggestive of personal probabilities, two keepers walked their prisoner past us in the darkness. Not twenty yards away one set up a shout, inquiring the success of the carefully-laid trap.

'We've got the lot!' sounded from across the water—a reply which relieved us in so far as we now thought no especial watch was being kept for us. It was a long, weary time before the poacher signified that it was safe to proceed.

Down the slimy rocks we descended as silently as possible, drawing towards the head of the long trough. You may be sure that we kept a very sharp lookout as we moved into the half-light of the riverbed, but neither sight nor sound of lurking danger was there. At a sign I turned my shaft of light on the clear waters ; the poacher, selecting his salmon, struck unerringly, and the fish was bagged. Again I showed the light, but, though the leister poised, the stroke was never made, for up to the gloomy sky another signal tore. This was for us in very deed.

'Into t' water,' cried the poacher, 'or we're caught!'

There was no time for contemplating the darkling stream, or for shivering on the brink —the terror of the police-court is mightily great. In the three of us stepped; knee-deep the cold was horrible, waist-deep the feeling was worse, but before bottom was touched the water was neck-high, and the chill seemed to freeze our very marrow. The poacher we still had confidence in, for he had been in scores of similar tight corners; with arms outstretched he pressed us close to the rocky bank, which for six feet almost overhung. When the rocket stars had faded away, I noticed a light travelling along the water and the further bank upstream; the keepers apparently knew we had not resorted to the woods, and were examining the rocky brink. I heard them moving high above our heads, and saw the gleam of lanterns light up the running waters almost within arm's length, then pass on without a pause. The chill of the water was forgotten in that breathless five minutes, but it was again racking us when the poacher said:

'Now we're safe for a bit. Sink that salmon bag with a couple of stones, and we'll make downstream.'

The three of us were fair swimmers, so made little of the distance to the foot of the trough, where, emerging, we crawled cautiously up the bank, and by devious ways passed through the wood. Though chilled through and through, we still had escaped capture, for which we were thankful.

The fish! Oh, our poacher must have found his way again to the pool ere daybreak and rescued the sunken bag, for our landlady came to us at breakfast—a fine piece of salmon was on the table—bustling with information.

'Do you see that salmon? Well, what do you think? I found a whole big fish hanging up in the cart-house, with all the cats on the farm watching it, first thing this morning. The keepers must have run some poacher very hard before he left his fish like that.'

Needless to say, the good lady was unaware that we had spent our night otherwise than in sleep, and that two wet suits of clothes were being surreptitiously dried behind a pile of sacks in the boiler-house.

TALES OF THE MIST

TALES OF THE MIST

JOHN BENNETT, the doyen of English fell guides, gives the following as one of his most arduous experiences :

'I left Dungeon Ghyll one wet afternoon guiding a party to Scawfell Pike. At the top of Rossett Ghyll one of the ladies was too tired to go further. I did not wish to leave her without a companion, but she insisted that all the others should complete their walk. We left her resting by a large boulder, and soon were out of sight in the mist. A couple of hours later we returned, but there was no trace of the lady. As it was very probable she had already returned to the hotel, this circumstance did not then trouble us much. But when we got home the lady had not been seen, so I set out again up the ghyll to Esk Hause, and there turned down the head into Borrowdale, as it was apparent that the lady had somehow strayed from the path. At Seathwaite,

Seatoller, and Rosthwaite I visited all the inns and outlying houses; then, still unsuccessful, turned up the pass to Wastdalehead.

'After a seven-mile tramp through very dense cloud, I came to old Will Ritson's, but could hear of no visitor. I ascended Scawfell Pike, and searched closely and unavailingly as I returned. The lads of the dalehead had been out scouring the hillsides in the meantime, and I got in just after they had completed their task. It was now past midnight and a wild night. After some supper—not many in the hotel would go to bed that night—I made another attempt, almost in despair. There was not the slightest answer to my calls. I climbed over to Eskdale, hoping that my lady had found her way there, and with the intention of raising the alarm thoroughly. At about four o'clock I knocked at the Woolpack, near Boot, and was told that a lady in a very exhausted condition had struggled to the door three hours before. She was then in a dead faint, but I was speedily satisfied that my weary hunt was finished.

'It appeared that the lady, feeling a little less tired, had followed from Rossett Ghyll less than an hour after we left her. For a while she had followed the path with ease, then lost it completely. Whilst trying to find it again among the mist, she became hopelessly confused as to direction, crossed streams, climbed and descended huge rocks, and walked over much rough ground. At length she found herself by a fence, and, following this a good way, saw the lights of the Woolpack in the distance.'

Such an incident is not uncommon even in these days, when mountain-paths are so well worn that any stranger may keep on them. But even if the route be lost, there is little peril to anyone who knows the fells. The only real awkward possibility that I know of is the danger of coming without warning upon a precipitous descent. Nearly every accident recorded is due to the fact that most people in such a predicament attempt to descend the face of the crag, often coming to grief. On one of his thirty or forty annual ascents of Helvellyn, for the purpose of measuring the density of its atmosphere at various altitudes, John Dalton and his companions suddenly found themselves enveloped in a dense cloud, which had swept up and closed round them unawares. They attempted to move, and stepped a few feet in advance, holding by the skirts of each other's coat, when the old philosopher suddenly drew back, saying: 'Not a step more! There is nothing but cloud to tread on!' It was true; their unconscious feet were on the very edge of the precipice which plunges sheer down to Red Tarn.

To those who know the fells, abundant indications give warning of the nearness of a precipice, as well as, if the route be more familiar, to determine exactly the position of the rambler. These signs are in the air; the different notes sounded by the wind to right and left are of great value. A breeze rushing up or along a wide expanse of grass has a seething note in it, whereas if rising suddenly from a deep dalehead, and encountering many crags, there is a harsh roar in the sound. Once when wandering along Helvellyn, our only proof that we had not involuntarily taken a wrong direction—by no means unusual in a dense mist—was the rattle of the wind among the cliffs on the Patterdale side of the mountain. The edge of a precipice is always heralded by a line of outcroppings, and when travelling in the mist watch should always be kept for these.

A shepherd of my acquaintance started from Wastdalehead one wet afternoon to reach a farm in the Grasmere Valley. His proper route was by Styehead Pass to Esk Hause, thence to Angle Tarn, when a short cast to the left would bring him to the caërn at Stakepasshead. A direct north-easterly course from here would bring him home. However, after leaving the tarn he failed to touch the caërn, but, keeping on for an hour, he came across the splintered edges of projecting strata among the short bent-grass. He guessed that he was too far north, and standing by a craggy slope of Wythburndale. When, however, the hill seemed to turn back on his route, he knew that something was amiss.

The wind, happily, was now blowing the masses of mist away, and every minute the light increased. When the air cleared sufficiently, the shepherd found himself standing on the brink of Pavey Ark, a tremendous array of scree and cliff adjoining Langdale Pikes, with the tarn of Stickle brooding 1,200 feet below, some six miles from his supposed position. Had he carried out the intention of descending, which he formed on approaching the edge, he would have undoubtedly gone into serious danger. Indeed, three years later a fatal accident occurred at the very same point.

The liability of tourists to go astray among the misty clouds is great, and one of the few exciting incidents of dalehead life is to be called upon to join in a search. The number of such hunts, however, does not represent the total of 'losts.' Parties or individuals working from some hotel, and starting with the avowed intention of returning the same evening, or sending their luggage beforehand to another hotel, purposing to follow by a more or less circuitous route, are easily missed. But the Bohemian of the fells, who defines to himself no route, is seldom traced. A couple of visitors to the Lake District arranged to walk from Dungeon Ghyll and Grasmere respectively, to meet on the fells near Sergeant Man. The day was very wet and misty, but the man from Grasmere reached the rendezvous, and, after waiting a long time, pushed on to Dungeon Ghyll, where he found that his friend had started, as arranged, some hours previously. The tourist searched the way carefully over to Grasmere, where he stated the circumstances to the inhabitants. Evening was fast drawing on, and everyone turned out to the quest. Not till the last gleam of light faded from the skies did the wearied parties return, when at his hotel the Grasmere tourist found a telegram from his friend, stating that, after climbing into the mist, he had changed his mind and struck along the hillside to Windermere. Many tourists, when lost in the mist, try to await the raising of the cloud curtain. Certainly this is the safest method, but the fog-banks close in for days at times, and human endurance is limited. A gentleman and his sister staying at Mardale essayed to climb Kentmere High Street one misty day. Soon after reaching the shoulder of the ridge, however, they got into difficulties, and finally, lest worse should befall, decided to wait. They were missed from the hotel, and the proprietor with two or three helpers took different tracks up the mountain. After three hours' search, the couple, now half frozen with the chilly mist, were rescued.

The Scarf Gap district, near Buttermere, with its many rocky hillocks of almost similar contour, is well known in misty weather for 'circular walking.' Some years ago a party of ladies going from Wastdalehead to Buttermere were unexpectedly caught in the mist here. For hours they wandered about the fellsides. One of the ladies dropped her pocket-book, and recovered it again about two hours later—conclusive proof that they had been walking in a circle. It is pleasant to add that when the mist lifted, just before sunset, this party found themselves quite close to the path they had so long and utterly lost.

Though we have many times had the pleasure of walking on the fells during dense mists, we have never had the temerity to go crag-climbing under such conditions. The rocks are usually very slippery, and a false step at any point of a steep climb would be fatal. There is little danger of losing your way among the rocks if, in the first place, you correctly hit off the entrance of the climb, but that is difficult when there are many similar openings in the cliff. Once fairly on the right track, however, you can follow the route marked by the white scratches of the hobnails of your predecessors. The mist, though burying any distant landmark, seldom interferes with your view of the work close at hand. People there are, however, who are dead to all discomfort, and who on occasion go climbing even in the densest mist, and the account of an ascent of the Napes Needle, a familiar crag on Great Gable, will be of interest :

'As the weather was uncompromising and I wanted an easy day, I strolled out for a solitary scramble towards the Napes rocks, to make a mere bowing acquaintance with the Needle, and with the virtuous intention of doing nothing rash in the way of venturing upon a single-handed attack upon it. At the moment of leaving the grass and taking to the rocks, I stepped into cloudland, and there came on a miserable drizzle that was not far removed from rain. There was nothing for it but to get wet. No one can climb in a waterproof, even though it be only a cape ; and as to any other protection against the weather, you may as well offer mackintoshes to a family of otters. Somewhere up above was the Needle, but whether I had passed the place or not I could not tell. So I ensconced myself in a sort of cave among some huge boulders to consider the plan of campaign with the aid of a quiet pipe, and had almost given it up as a bad job and made up my mind to return, when I heard voices through the mist. Setting up a halloo, and getting a response, I shouted : " Is the Needle up there?" " Yes, we're on it—come up," was the answer. I had been sitting all the time at its very base ; so up I went, and, scrambling up a steep but easy gully, soon gained the narrow rock-platform a few feet below the crack which marks the beginning of the climb of the Needle. I found here two first-rate climbers who had just been to the summit of the rock, and were discussing lunch. They very kindly expressed their willingness to go up again if I wanted to make the ascent.

'Here was a chance not to be lost, so I gladly accepted their offer, and we were soon roped and ready : R—— the leader, I middle man, and M—— came last. The ascents were very difficult, and with muscles out of training for a gymnastic feat such as mounting the last piece of the slippery rock—comparable only to climbing and adhering to a narrow mantelshelf—I was glad to avail myself of a "shoulder-up." Accordingly, M—— crouched down on the narrow cornice, and, stepping with my left foot on to his right shoulder, I mounted in sybaritic fashion on to the ledge. The mist was boiling up all around us, so that we could see the foot of the rock-shaft, and R——, who ought to have known much better, shouted just as I was making the dangerous step up: "Come, hurry up down there! this beastly weather makes me think of sunnier climes." Sidling along, I found round the corner of rock a jutting ledge eighteen inches higher that offered a good hold for both feet. The next foothold was for the left foot —a small projection about an inch wide, and several inches higher on the face of the rock. This was about the most ticklish part of the whole climb. It is necessary to step with the left foot confidently up on to this projection, which slopes slightly the wrong way. To make a false step in doing so might entail serious consequences, as the hand-support is of the slightest. A boot edged with good ice-nails would get a firm grip on the projecting ledge, but my boots were merely studded, and the round leather edge felt insecure enough on the wet and smooth stone. However, the step was successfully accomplished, and I was then able easily to grip the right hand and top edges of the boulder in close embrace. A final pull-up, and I lay on my chest across the summit, and after a gasp of relief drew my legs up after me.'

In winter the mists are horrible. I don't suppose many of my readers have ever crossed the desolate, snow-covered uplands. It is dreary enough work when the pallid sun glints along the even surface, lighting up the air with an unwonted shimmer, and the great crags loom out on the fell-sides. The passes between Buttermere and Wastdalehead—Scarf Gap and Black Sail—may be a case in point. As the snow is crunched up towards the narrow depression from which the former is named, the darkness of the afternoon increases. A foot of snow has already obliterated the path, and it now seems apparent that there will be a further fall. In a second the sky seems to fall around us. We barely feel the extra chilliness of the air before the scene is darkened with falling particles, and we look around to find ourselves immured in the gray cloud-walls. A circle of twenty yards of uneven snow is all we can see, the view of lake and mountain being alike blotted out. Perhaps for ten minutes we did not realize the danger of our position, but soon after crossing the ridge towards Ennerdale it dawned on us. Now, however, retreat was more difficult than advance. With every danger-signal masked, with the path lost and undiscoverable, and the wind sending the white storm full in our faces, our position was one of most extreme discomfort. We threw away all idea of getting near the caërns and huts at the foot of Black Sail, devoutly hoping to reach the valley bottom in safety. Drifts of various depths had to be struggled through, and descents of screes and moraines of boulders negotiated. It was a most anxious time. A slip on one of those abrupt breasts of snow might end with us, as with more than one other wanderer of the fell, in a broken leg. How some poor fellows must have suffered before death's kindly sleep fell upon them! Unable to get away, perhaps with their poor tortured limbs jammed between immovable boulders, they had simply to freeze or to starve. By carefully following the deepest drifts, we got on to a corner of rock whence all but a thin coating of snow had been whirled by the wind. It was no precipice, and, though the descent was hard work indeed, we could yet see our way, and found this route much preferable. We got into daylight again at the head of Ennerdale Valley, and stayed an hour there in the old hut, while the snowstorm passed. There was nothing to make a fire of, and we were glad to note the clearing of the pass in front. We just got over the top of Black Sail before the clouds closed again behind us.

BY THE SHORE

BY THE SHORE

I. DAYBREAK ON THE SANDS

THE great mass of the limestone head bounding our estuary to the southward loomed black and sullen against the delicate pearl clouds, through which an unseen sun was endeavouring to diffuse some measure of day to our little valley. To seaward the tide had receded far, and the chill white lines of water tossed to the wind beyond a wide stretch of sand. To landward the dun mist of morning hung, blotting out the distant hills and the woodlands, leaving in view only a stretch of marshy pastures and the houses of a tiny village. Though we were early astir, yet others were in advance; the fishermen were going to take up the spoils which night had brought to the nets fixed on the sand-banks.

*   *   *   *   *

At eventide a great flock of wild-duck of various kinds settled after their long flight from

the northward upon the moving waters of the
bay. They were hungry, but much noise had
been heard as they winged over the fishing-village.
At nightfall it would be safe to venture closer,
and, besides, there would be precious little food
to be delved out of those adamant sands, from
which the water had long been absent. The
flock thus sat on the tossing waters awhile, resting. Then a few detached themselves from the
main body, and floated shoreward with the wash
of the tide. They were scouts, to spy out the
safest ground for feeding. Out beyond the
gray stump of the ruined Pile, once fort and
port in one, a fiery strip of cloud was losing its
glow, turning slowly to crimson and to violet,
after which it lost all that distinguished it from
its vapour neighbours. In the east perhaps the
moon had risen, for, though the great light was
withdrawn, a visibility still reigned. The scouts
thrown out by the cloud of duck floated up with
the incoming tide awhile, then turned from its
current into the slack waters widening into a pool
near the mouth of a creek. Here, after a cautious
survey of their surroundings, they settled down to
feed.

Meanwhile the main body had felt the rising
pulsations of Mother Ocean, and, like an innumerable flotilla of tiny strange craft, they, too,

had been approaching with the inflowing stream. In the soft sand were numerous worms and molluscs, and those tiny atoms of life which duck assimilate with avidity. In the faint luminosity prevailing, whether from a clouded moon or the natural light on the water, their movements were plainly visible. A duck floating on the surface would suddenly dip its head beneath the water; then deeper and deeper it went, till the main part of its body was submerged, and the tail and a pair of wildly-moving web-feet were all that remained in sight. Further seaward the duck dived down clean out of sight after the food they were in such need of, coming up to the surface for a moment, shaking their heads and necks clear of water, then disappearing in a flash again. Other birds, more fastidious, maybe, followed in the rising waters, and never dipped deeper than their neck-length. The duck feeding with peaceable cutterings to one another made a pretty sight; yet, unknown to the casual observer, a grim tragedy was occurring right in his sight. Bird after bird dived down and never rose to sight again. The deep-water feeders gave no sign as their numbers were diminished by the score; odd birds feeding in middle depths might have been seen to splash a little as their tails and web-feet were gradually covered by the rising water, while among the shore-haunters there was occasionally a little commotion. Birds were being suffocated on all sides, yet the survivors heedlessly went on gorging, till—— For, pegged flat along the sand-banks, the fishermen had left their nets, ready for the ground-loving flocks which would come up with the tide. The duck, in diving and 'grobbling' about for their food, got their heads so firmly fixed among the meshes of the nets that they could not withdraw them again, and so were slowly done to death.

*　　*　　*　　*　　*

Not every one of the village fishermen had got out to his nets. We could hear a ramshackle cart coming clattering down the stony lane behind us. Immediately the belt of shingle was passed, the solitary figure in the vehicle put the horse to its best trot over the swelling sands. It was old Jack, the man whose nets were planted furthest seaward, and it behoved him to move quickly, lest the tide should again cover them before he had taken his toll of their contents. As we rambled further and further out, the shore seemed to rise in altitude, and the great crag where a brave knight slew the last wolf in the countryside seemed to raise its bulk to a more commanding height. In front of us the fishermen's carts were still far away, and across the channel daylight showed us the chimneys of a town, backed by a long sharp line of hills. In half an hour we reached the nearest cart. Looking into it, we saw a great mass of scales and feathers—the fish and the duck ensnared during the night. This man had completed clearing his net, and was busily pegging it down to the sand-bed, ready for another tide. We would dearly have liked to examine his load, but the man was too feverishly at work ; therefore we looked around to see who had not yet completed their task, and, of course, first thought of the old man who in his cart had passed up a while ago. After a moment's consideration, we decided to go as far as the point where his nets were, and to watch him empty them. A stiff breeze was blowing across the estuary, and helped us to run along to the old man's netting-ground more easily. He looked up at our approach, and asked us to lend a hand, as the tide had turned and time was precious. My friend and I, therefore, got to work, jerking the fish and fowl clear of the meshes into baskets, which were emptied into the body of the cart in one con-fused mass. 'There isn't time to sort them,' we agreed with reluctance. In maybe ten minutes we had half filled the cart, and stood watching the fisherman repegging down his nets. The breeze soughed coldly across the bleak sands, the sting of the frozen Northland in it, while the soft rush as the white rollers broke nearer and nearer on the sand-bank filled our ears. The old man directed us to assist in stretching the nets. 'Be sharp!' he said, without a glance at the fast-incoming tide. The last rope was stretched and the last peg driven, and the sea was roaring in a great stream not a hundred yards away. 'Into t' cart, and sharp!' And on the instant we obeyed.

I had not looked landward for some time, and was surprised to find that our spit of sand was now cut off by a slowly-widening arm of the sea. If this was deep and we could not cross it in the cart, if it became furrowed with strong water and our cart was overwhelmed, then we would be in a dangerous strait; for swimming in the chill waters of a December tide is not to be contemplated without misgiving. But old Jack, with a word of encouragement to his horse, drove straight at the water. My feelings as I looked over the side of the cart were uneasy, and I watched the water rise upward from wheel-rim, by the thin spokes, to the axle, and higher and higher, till I heard it wash in the bottom of the cart around my feet. Our horse was plodding steadily away, though breast-deep in the tide. Deeper we sank, and deeper still, till our spoil of the nets was hidden in the flood, and the horse's head and a strip of its back was all that was visible of it. Still on the game old animal steadily waded, and it became apparent that the perils of the passage were over. Immediately we came on to firm sand, old Jack leapt off the shaft on which he had stood, and called us to get out.

'Now we must run for it. The water 'll be pretty deep just outside the shingles.'

The old mare appreciated this remark as well, for it broke into its best lumbering trot, dragging the lightened cart, from which the sea-water oozed, at a fairish pace, to which we three kept up. A quarter of a mile in front was the shore, but a fast-running tongue of sea-water cut us off. Again we mounted the cart as the water was touched, and the blue-jerseyed fisherman drove straight ahead. I was not prepared for what now followed. A powerful undertow whirled us—cart, horse, and men—bodily seaward, while the swift stream striking the oaken sides of the vehicle threw spray right over us. But old Jack had been cautious in his selection of a point to pass the current, and the eddy of the fierce undertow brought the horse where it could take footing again, after which it speedily drew up into safety.

Of course, our first action, after changing our soaking clothes, was to examine the load of duck and flooks we had helped to bring to land. I had prepared myself for disappointment, but surely these damp, muddy, ruffled balls of feathers were not the same as the brightly-coloured, carefully-

preened uniform of the ducks which had swum to
the sand-banks when the moon was clouded o'er
last night? The varieties we had looked to see—
the scaup, the teal, the widgeon, etc.—were hardly
distinguishable to our novice eyes, and ere long we
gave up the attempt in despair. But one bird did
interest us, and that was a neat-feathered northern
diver, which is a rarity to the fishermen. As to
the others, we did not feel it incongruous to their
estate to hear them hawked about in the adjacent
town that afternoon by old Jack to a sing-song
of—

'Fine fresh flooks alive, alive'oh!
    Alive oh, alive oh!
Fine fresh flooks alive, alive oh!
    Alive oh, alive oh!
Now, my old lasses, come out with your dishes,
And I'll fill you them full for a trifle.'

II. The Peril of the Sands

ONE incident in the life of George Moore of Cumberland has always struck my imagination, and that is his narrow escape from drowning when crossing Morecambe Bay by the oversands route.

Outside the estuaries of the rivers Kent, Leven and Winster, sand-banks stretch almost level seaward for miles, and as the tides recede these soon become clear of water, and in the course of an hour have settled so firmly in most parts that heavy traffic may readily pass. And from the days of Roman legions marching across till the era of railways this was the crossing preferred by all traffic to and from Furness and West Cumberland. The way was fraught with dangers : sometimes a strong wind from the south-west held back the ebbing of the waters for an hour or more, and forced up the succeeding 'flow' long before the normal time. On many a stormy day the rush of a single comber blotted out, with a depth of blue water, acres of bare sand. Any conveyance midway on its journey would be simply washed away with such an eight-foot wave ; horses and men encountered would be borne over without chance of escape. The channels of the rivers, being below the general sand-level, also constituted a peril. The banks were constantly crumbling under the action of salt water and fresh, and the direction and depth of the current at any given point varied much from tide to tide. At a point where last ebb the eau or river of the sea was fordable, now there might be a deep cavity filled with water, in which, should the driver venture, horse and man and conveyance might be easily lost. That such a thing has happened over and over again is the story told by hundreds of epitaphs in the burying-places of the surrounding countrysides. The third danger was that of quicksand—a terribly remorseless enemy to the traveller ; while in misty weather and during the hours of darkness it was possible to lose all sense of direction over the bewildering level waste, and to guide your horse, perhaps, straight out to sea. Case after case could be cited of men going several miles out of their courses from such an accident: the number of mysterious drownings on the sands never to be properly traced gives the impression that those who escape after such mistakes are in a terrible minority.

BY THE SHORE

George Moore reached Cartmel towards evening. He did not take time to inquire as to the state of the tide, but drove off at once towards the sands. It was a reckless undertaking, as he soon found out, for he was scarcely halfway across before he saw the tide was turning. The man who was with him in the carriage jumped out and went back. But George, believing that he was on the right track, drove on. The water was now approaching like a mill-race. He flogged his horses as he never flogged them before. The sand shifted beneath their feet, so he turned aside and drove where foothold still held. A mirage rose before him, and he seemed to see the land. But it disappeared and reappeared again and again. The situation became terrible.

At length he heard a loud shout from some person to the left. One of the mounted guides had seen his peril. The man spurred his horse into the water, suddenly turned round, and waved him to come onward in that direction. Moore understood his position at once, and pulled his horses round by sheer force towards land. By dint of flogging and struggling the horses at length touched the ground, dragged the carriage up the sands, and Moore's life was saved.

Other equally exciting incidents occur to me as I write. Once the mail-coach when far out on

265

the sands was struck by a powerful gust of wind, and blown bodily some hundred yards out of its course, where it capsized. The horses and passengers made for the shore as quickly as possible. Some days later the great vehicle was found near the tideway, and, after re-upholstering, was again put in use.

The dangers of the sands were so well known from the earliest times that the abbeys, and after their dissolution the Crown, were charged to maintain men whose duty it was to vigilantly study the tideway and conduct passengers safely across. The post of guide on the Kent sands was held by one family for over five hundred years.

During my wanderings in the districts near the sands, I have come across many who had stories to tell of perils braved or witnessed. What more perilous than to have, when your cart is far from shore, a wheel break under a sudden strain put upon it. Yet this happened when a family, some quite young children, was crossing the Leven sands. Two men set out for the nearest village to have the breakage repaired, leaving the women and children to make the best of it during the chilly night. It was several hours before the repair was completed, the tide had long turned, and the wheel was fixed against time. The delayed cart was saved with difficulty, for so high had the water risen that the horses were almost swept off their feet by the force of waves which again and again broke against the carts.

The story is told of a funeral crossing the sands being caught up by the tide ; the coffin had to be temporarily left to the mercy of the seas. Another cortège, when halfway across, had to hasten to the shelter of Holme Island—not then, as now, connected with the mainland by a causeway—and from the rocky shores of this they watched the raging sea close over their tracks. More than once the mail-coach has struggled to this refuge when, after passing one of the river channels, the other was, through a sudden rise of the tide, found unfordable, and advance or retreat by the direct route was equally impossible.

But the narrative of one who crossed the sands in his early years—the old man has been dead some years now—is, even among such episodes as already mentioned, worth placing on record :

' It was mid-afternoon when the gentleman for whom I was working as groom decided to pass from Lancaster to Ulverston. The month was February, and a faint griming of snow covered the land. The day had been hazy, and the weather-wise said a storm was brewing in a villainous-looking patch of clouds hanging out to sea. Of course I had to go, though I urged the undesirability of driving the horses through the cold waters of the channel. At half-past four we were at Hest Bank, having driven quickly over the frozen roads.

' The folks at the inn advised us to stop there for the night, as it was growing dusk and the wind was rising. But on we went. The guide accompanied us to the Keer, and saw us safely across, then told us that by following a line of bushes planted in the sand we would in about a mile fall in with the Kent guide, who was mounted. We had scarce left this man, whose repeated warnings made me more uneasy, when from the sea there crept up a thick gray cloud, which so enveloped us that I had to dismount and lead the horses, for from our seats we could not see from one small tuft to another. I was thus puzzling out the route, when we came to a pool of water, at which the gray mare shied and then bolted. The loose rein was wrested from my hand, but as the carriage swept past I leapt and clutched the back. The horses ran for fully a minute—the distance was impossible to guess in the dusk of the cloud—before they could be stopped. And when at last they came to a standstill, imagine our plight! We were far out on those bleak sands without any knowledge as to where sound land lay; turn as we might, the open sea was a perilous thing to risk. The tide had turned, and would now be running in at a tremendous rate. Even should running waters be met with, these would give no clue as to direction, for they might be a river-current or a mere eddy of the waves. Then, too, the wind was rising higher, and from afar we heard the growling roar of the sea. "What shall we do?" said the master. I would not reply. The moment of indecision in his mind passed, and he continued: "John, this is one way to die. Let us drive onward somewhere. If so be that we take a wrong turning, it will be but a quicker ending." I said now: "Let the horses try; they will turn for the land surer than we." Well, the horses had by this time in some manner realized the danger; they stood shivering and pawing the sands, looking first to seaward, whence the subdued thunder was proceeding, then at one another in silence askance, and to us. At the word they walked steadily forward, bearing, as it seemed to me, somewhat to the left. "If this direction is correct, God help us!" I thought. I spoke to them again, and they quickened to a trot. The sound of their rapid hoofs for a while drowned in my ears that dull, insistent roar, to which, as my senses indicated, we were gradually coming nearer and nearer.

Pool after pool of water was run into, but the horses were steady now.

'All this time the cloud had been blowing along the sands, never lifting a fathom, but allowing some three lengths' clear view ahead, and the wind blew still harder. Dusk it had been when we lost our way; it was almost pitch-dark now. Time and again I thought voices came through our enveloping shroud, but though I called often there was no reply. Sound did not carry far, and our loudest shouts seemed to be stifled on our lips. As I looked steadily ahead into the flurry of snowflakes, which accompanied a stiffer squall than usual, I thought the chestnut's ear twitched as though sensitive to something occurring not far away. Then the gray cheered up—it had been doggedly pressing against the collar for some time, as though the previous terror had sapped its strength—and I turned to the master at my elbow. His face was lit with expectation, tempered with doubt. He forestalled my question. "Do you see that? I have been watching for a few seconds, though I didn't speak, for fear it might be a delusion." But our animals broke into a canter, and shortly the air around us was filled with the sounds of cracking whips and shouting men; and it didn't take more than a second for us to realize that we had fallen in with a band of carriers laden with goods for the Ulverston market. Where we had been in our perilous wandering will never be known, but we returned to safety quite close to where the Kent was to be crossed. The carriers had planned to stay the night at Cartmel, and to cross the Leven sands after the morning tide, so we stayed in their company. During the night, however, the threatening storm burst; and at daybreak the sea in the channel raged so wildly that not one would venture, and all made the détour over hilly roads to Newby Bridge, and so to our journey's end.'

SPORT AMONG THE FELLS

SPORT AMONG THE FELLS

I. Along the Heather

IT is always with exhilaration that the sportsman hears the first wing-rush of the season, and sees his first covey of grouse whirl along the heathery waste. The gun is thrown up, and on the instant the bird is singled. At the report a few feathers are struck up from the winger. Almost instantly the fury of its pinionings ceases, its flight droops, and becomes more and more unsteady, till with a thud it reaches the grass just as your retriever gets within distance.

In our district of rough shootings, the twelfth is the only festival the gunner observes, for the grouse is our stable game-bird. But though restricted in its variety of sport, ours, also, is one of the few areas in which genuine old-fashioned shooting is to be had. The exigencies of falling revenues has stopped the heavy stocking and close preserving formerly the custom, and our birds are almost always wild—wild with the freedom of the spreading moorland, not with the wildness of terror. Beating is rarely resorted to by the occupiers of our shootings, for men are scarce in upland valleys.

The evening of the eleventh closed down over the steeps in lurid fashion, and at dark a storm was whistling along the near-by braes. Our keeper, however, held that by sunrise the worst of the tempest would be spent, and that a clear day was in store for us. However, when we arose the gale still shrieked along the uplands, driving huge banks of cloud before it. The rain had ceased some hours before, but every dell was occupied with a roaring flood, and the bosky places were palpably saturated. The keeper, who appeared to have spent the whole of the wild night patrolling the only route by which poachers could reach the moor, was decidedly of opinion that, bad as the weather was, it was still improving rapidly. The clouds, whirling ghostlike in the uncertain light, were less frequent, and did not fall so far down the slopes. Now and again the surf of billowy white passed clear of the fellside for a few seconds.

Up and be doing was advised; and, as we were in friendly rivalry with the holders of the other moors as to whose gun should fall the earliest bird of the season, in a few seconds we were striding through the woods, listening to the eerie voice of the gale in the reeling pine-tops, or to the gushing down secluded ghylls of creamy torrents.

In ten minutes we were on the bleak moor; the pressure of the wind was so strong that we could barely keep our feet. The grass was beaded with raindrops; the tangled bushes through which here and there we had to force a passage shook drenching showers upon us. Walking along some half-mile, we got into the shelter of a great rib of mountain; and here the keeper anticipated sport. So far not a bird had stirred, or even called; whether they had deserted the exposed brae or were unwilling to rise, I cannot say.

Now, looking across the deep, narrow valley, we espied at a great distance another shooting-party passing through the heather in extended line. Our keeper chuckled:

' T' Ferns folk'll not git t' first birrd to-day '

I was not so certain, for I had seen two wee puffs of smoke rise from the centre of their line. But though the slow advance checked, there was no crowding together to congratulate a successful first shot.

The presence of rivals spurred us on, but, try as we would, not a bird could be found in the wet, quiet hollow; then, worse than all, a fine gray veil drew itself between us and our distant view, growing rapidly more dense, till we could see but a few yards.

'Ferns wins,' groaned I; but the ever-confident Jack claimed that it would require a finer shot than any of theirs to down a bird on that gusty moor. 'But what of the flukes—eh?'

'We've as much chance as they. Keep a sharp lookout as we come opposite to these screes, and fire at the first thing that moves.'

Of course, this was what we were bound to do. In a few minutes the cloud blew aside, and just as its final skirts were rushing from the heather and scree in front, up rose with wild clamouring a covey of grouse. There was a sharp crackle as four guns belched forth together on them. Down went three birds. Whose was the first? Well, each claimed the honour, but the gamekeeper, as final referee, laid down that when shots are simultaneous the order of birds reaching the ground must count. The scene of this informal court was dramatic: the weathered old man, his kindly face lit up with delight at our referring the matter to him; the three splendid dusky-red birds laid neatly in front; the dogs wandering around, probably contrasting this delay with our usual pushing habits; and our four faces showing varying degrees of anxiety as we awaited the veteran's decision. For a minute he sat silent and motionless, his gray-clad body standing out against the dark heather and gray-lichened crag of the rolling, windy moor, and when his first point was again agreed to, he declared that the cock was the first down. As I was the only one who had singled him, it was *my first grouse*.

Now half an hour more we waited for better light, with a possible lifting of the mist-curtain sufficiently high for sport to be more than intermittent. And after a while things certainly began to be brighter. As we patrolled along, the birds rose better and the guns got into better use. But all day the wind remained powerful enough to aid the birds' escape.

Another year the circumstances of shooting were easier, the weather was fine, our stock promising, and our first bird was got very early. One of the dogs ranging in very delight in front flushed a small covey from a dot of heather just beyond the garden palings, and our youngest gun dropped a straggler. The chances of a kill at the long range were so remote that no one else attempted a shot.

Than the moors on a fine September morning I cannot conceive a fairer space. At midsummer the bees drone sleepily over the blooming heather, the little runnels murmur distantly from their grass-hidden courses. Of bird-life little is to be seen; the grouse cower among the heather until near sundown. As we stand by the weedy tarn this morning, however, there is ample evidence that the spreading mantle of chocolate and green is thronged with life. Here the path crosses a boggy tract where dirty jets of water spurt over our boots; now we encounter bouldery ground, and the path winds among the greater fragments. Anon we brush through a narrow channel running athwart a waste of heather.

'There they go!' There is a sharp rustle among the grass, some hurried wing-beats and a hoarse call 'come-back, come-back,' and a splendid covey of grouse sail away from us. But not a gun is raised, for the gamekeeper has expressly stipulated that in this basin of green swamp and sparkling dot of water, chosen haunt at all times of wild-duck, not a shot is yet to be fired. Regretfully we trudge upward on the rugged path to the top of the slope.

Now the dogs are released, and the line of guns shakes out. The old keeper, as a special favour in return for early summer inquiries about his broods, walks close beside, constituting himself my loader. I know this moor well; for several years I have watched the seasons pass over its face of spreading bracken and stiff, erect heather; otherwise I might be impatient.

'It's a bit noisy for t' birds here,' is an apology hazarded by the old man; 'a good many sheep have been driven across there this last week. ('Across there,' indicated by a sweep of his arm, is a moorland road, lonesome-looking enough to-day.)

A gun is discharged at the far end of our line— I cannot see exactly by whom, as we are in a slight fold of the moor, then quite a small volley. A covey has flown right down the line of guns. In a moment the birds whir across my line of vision, but they are too far away for a shot. This glen illumined by the morning sunshine is like a piece from fairyland. Sphagnum in all stages, golden and white and green, and gray-green bent; tinkling streamlets and moss-hung rocks; every blade of grass, every branchlet of heather, every frond of fern and bracken, is decked with beads of dew, and the sunshine revels in each and every drop as though it were a crystal prism, throwing off glories and halos of rainbow hues.

In a minute we clear this little gully and are again level with the others. Each man carries his own game-bag (save myself, whom the veteran serves), and will do his own loading; but game is sparse, and for five brace apiece we may have to tramp as many miles. However, there is always magnificent scenery and bracing air, and now and again there will be lively incidents—sequences of shots as rapid as you can fire and exchange shells. 'Nerves' on such occasions are almost sure to leave you with an empty game-bag.

So along we tramp, shooting where any opportunity arises. The dogs go through their work thoroughly and cheerfully ; we guns are young and athletic, so that the long walk does not tire us. At lunch-time we are close to a disused sheepfold, in the lee of which our meal is spread. During the half-hour rest we indulged in we got the old keeper to tell us stories from his own experience. He has been on various estates, and commanded all sorts of shooting ; but with middle age the homing instinct turned him to the land of the fells and lakes again. He had amassed what was to him a competency, but his hands could not drop the gun altogether, and he gladly accepted his present position—a lucrative pleasure, not a labour to him. And this was the story he told us, between puffs of a black clay pipe, as he sat on a lichened stone with his back against the wall of the sheepfold :

'Many years ago, near one of the best shooting estates in the Fells Country, there lived two poachers. Their ancestors had been frugal and thrifty, so that a small farm—twenty or thirty acres, maybe—and a cottage were left to these two. To meet them on the country roads or in their fields, they were simple, slow-speaking farmers like their neighbours. But to see them making nets and snares when the storm howled round the little house — as I have done—they were smart craftsmen. And in the dark woods and leas, or by the salmon streams, the most alert watcher could never find Dick and Ned. They could thread the worst-tangled glades without a sound, for they knew every inch of them. As to game, whether fin, fur, or feather, Dick and Ned were sure somehow to get a large share of it. Their house and bit of land lay between two wide sheep-farms. Their only sister had died when the lads were sixteen, their parents some time before, and after that bereavement the only companions they took were a dog and a cat. Concerning which there is a story.

' The two men were sat at breakfast, when Dick said, in his chanting voice :

' " Ned, thoo likes thy dog."

' " Dick, thoo likes thy cat."

' And at this the two joined battle. And when at last a chance caller at the house intervened and drew them apart, both men were dripping with blood. As quickly as they had fought they fell back to the old intimate intercourse, Ned alone remarking :

'"Well, ah'll hae to kill thee some day, Dick, and ah'll might as weel ha' done it noo."

'They were always like that, a word and a blow, till the keepers for miles around were almost all afraid of them, and purposely timed their beats to avoid the men. Ned, after a three months in gaol secured him by the old Lant Braithwaite, was one day working by a peat-pot [a bog-hole, generally partly filled with water], when that keeper came up and spoke cheerily to him. For reply, Ned—a stout man he was, and hard as an otter—gripped Lant, and after ten minutes' hard struggling threw him into the water. And, not content with that, the villain actually leapt with both feet on to the prostrate man's chest, and held him to suffocate beneath the shallow waters.

'Luckily, however, the struggle had been noticed by other men at work on the moor, and the poacher was by main force pulled away from a brutal murder. Of course, even in that slack time, when a policeman was never seen outside the county town, such a thing as this had to be looked into. Ned the poacher was arrested and thrown into prison. When he came before the magistrates, one of them hailed him with :

' " Well, Ned, Lant has got you again."

' " Ay, reet enough," was the off-hand reply; "but he wodn't [wouldn't] if ah'd hed t' peeat speead in me hand."

' What a present-day bench would say to a bloodthirsty address like this from a poacher, I don't know, but keepers' lives were held cheap in those days. Magistrates who would hang a man for stealing a sheep only inflicted a short sentence on the killer of a keeper. However, this time some big man took an interest in getting the poacher his due, and Ned finally got ten years' transportation.

' While he was away Dick was constantly in gaol. Perhaps he was less desperate than his brother, but I don't know. Two water-bailiffs once came upon him laden with salmon, fresh netted, on a bridge. They tried to arrest him, but he was a strong man, and threw first one and then the other over the ledge. It was a sheer forty feet, and a horrible flood was dashing through among the rocks. But if keepers were cheap, bailiffs were cheaper. Both men managed to struggle out of the torrent many yards lower down, one with a broken arm and a badly cut head, but nothing was said about it.

' Dick passed in and out of gaol till Ned's long term was up. One wild February morning the gray castle gate opened and the poacher walked out. He was a hardened and unforgiving beggar; for the first thing he said, as he fixed his eyes on the bleak sunrise, was:

'"Well, ah'm oot again, and noo Lant Braithwaite an' thoo be alive, I'll kill thee afore this time to-morn."

'At mid-day a great snowstorm closed down, and hourly became worse. At about four o'clock a knock came to Lant Braithwaite's door; it was opened by his grandson. An elderly, rough-looking man asked:

'"Whar's old Lant?"

'And the wide-eyed youngster replied: "Why, he's gone up ower t' fell-end to Tom Brackenrigg's. He wain't [will not] be back till varra laet [late]."

'"All right;" and the questioner, moving away out of the fold, was soon lost to view in the driving snow. After these long years Ned had at last located his victim, and now, with long-stored rage in his heart, he made up the snow-covered moorpath. "Me legs aren't as stiddy as they used to be," he muttered to himself, as he stuck fast and then collapsed into a deeper drift than usual. But, determined on his evil course, though he was still racked with weakness and gaol-fever, he straightened himself on to his feet and pushed on into the whirling blast.

'About the same time old Lant Braithwaite at the moorland farm threw down his hand of cards.

'"Bejocks, Jackie!" he said to his partner, "ah've clean forgitten to look at them traps doon be Blin' Tarn edge. Ah'll away."

'And, despite all arguments to stay, the old man—he was now upwards of seventy—set out. He spoke to a shepherd who was forcing his way against the seething gale to attend to his flock, and that was the last time he was seen alive. Next morning a search was made, and old Lant was found frozen stiff in the green copse you can see the tops of from here.'

'And the old poacher?' a voice queried.

'Ned was found dead, an awful baffled look on his face, crouched up among the heather just this side the ridge—near that big boulder above the beck course. Though within half a mile, he never found his enemy, after all.'

'And Dick?'

'Well, Dick hung about in a shiftless way for a while, then went clean away, and one fine morning, when the lilies bloomed among the rocks around, he was found drowned in the Fairy's Kail-pot down the next dale.'

As the old man concluded his gruesome story, he rose to his feet and whistled the dogs together. A minute later the line of guns was spreading anew across the moor. 'Watch for hares,' was the veteran's instructions, but, alas! puss is becoming rare with us, and we never saw a scrap of fur. The old keeper likes to have the harriers once a year across the moor, because, he says, as the visit is planned late, the noise scatters the birds, and prevents too much in-breeding. How far his idea is correct, I cannot of course say. The birds rise very slowly on this part of the moor, but they are strong, and your gun has to be deftly and rapidly used when they come.

'Stop!' said the old keeper suddenly, as we stood on a rise overlooking a tinkling streamlet. And as he spoke the dog in front flushed a bunch of birds from the outskirts of some heather. I fired rapidly, both barrels, and had the satisfaction of hitting each time. One bird was knocked over and over by the impact, and fell immediately, but the other on stiffening wings sailed away for thirty yards or so. The other members of the family with wild calls whirled out of sight over the next ridge.

'Quietly,' said the old man; 'we must have another shot at them.' And we had; before we had gone a hundred yards they rose in a bewildered, scattered flight, and, to my delight, down to the heather thumped another brace. These were my last shots that day, though we ranged the moor a couple of hours longer. The total bag averaged three brace per gun—not bad, considering the sparseness of game and the fact that two members of our party had discharged but a single cartridge apiece.

II. Rough the Beagle; or, A Rabbit-
shooting Expedition

THE morning was dull but clear. Behind us a lonely wayside station, with an overtowering background of mountains ; in front a grand piece of rolling country, with a far-away line of blue peaks. It was early October ; the march of autumn following on a wet summer had been so slow that as yet hardly a tree was shedding its leaves ; the hedgerows were dense and mostly green, and, as we passed from the road, the grass, both permanent and aftermath, was long and tangled. For a mile we walked by field-paths and through sunken lanes, spongy and rutted, damp with the exudations of countless hidden springs. Three of us, two gunsters and a rambler, and a dog. At the end of much seemingly aimless tramping we reached the boundary of the small shooting.

'Now,' said the principal to his fellow, 'you take those fields to the right, while I try around the marshy pasture on this side.'

I put the leash on the dog and followed with caution. Rough was black, white, and tan, and of the rough, genuine beagle type. There was nothing of the harrier or miniature foxhound about him. Also he was a show dog, with a proclivity for not looking his best on the correct occasions, therefore with his perfect shape and colour adding to his master's store of ' commended ' certificates.

Our premier gun was a slender, erect man, one who possessed a thorough knowledge of many kinds of outdoor sport, linked with a shrewd faculty for observation. He was a first-class shot. Means and manners of fur and feather by wood and water and lea were as an open book in his sight. Every nook and cranny of the two farms was known to him, and he had already reckoned out the possibilities of our day's work to a nicety. His companion, though keen on sport, was possessed of ' days.' At times he would bring off with ease almost marvellous shots, to fail on the following day in an almost elementary style. He was a well-set-up man and accustomed to work requiring organization and patience. Surely shooting rabbits as they run from feeding-ground to burrow would test this latter.

Down the dewy grass in the shadow of the hedge the principal stepped in silence, his gun

ready, watching and listening acutely for the rush
of the first rabbit. But it didn't come at present.
Rough walked steadily in the leash, and a moment
after was loosed. Away he went, ranging the
hedgesides thoroughly, but not a stray rabbit
could he find. All four fences of the small
pasture were visited. Rough's tail was indicative
of eager anticipation, but his tongue was silent.
Down the chief ditch where a patch of ragged-
robin grew he passed slowly, carefully. Rabbits
had been astir here, but not recently enough to
make the scents workable. We turned down a
ghyll, a declivity with steep grassy banks, just
before the other gun, with a rabbit dangling in his
hand, joined us from the other pastures.

The steep field to our right, bounded by thick
wattled hedges, was a known haunt, and dog,
guns, and the wanderer alike were on the alert.
But though we scanned the breadth of wind-
swept 'fog,' not the slightest indication of fur
was there. Rough, ranging down towards the
foot of the glen, began to quarter the tiny level
beneath the rise, and almost immediately up
jumped a big rabbit. For a few seconds its
rushing form was seen through the topmost ash-
stems fringing the stream which drained the ghyll ;
then, as it ran above them, there was a double
crack, both guns firing at once. The furry body

rolled over and over, then came to rest just as the pursuing Rough galloped up. Now, a beagle is not, like a trained retriever, to be commanded with a word at a moment like this. It runs up to its quarry, and, should it not be dead, worries it till satisfied. This penchant, though in Rough almost small enough to be innocent, caused one or other of us, after each shot, to 'pick up.'

A minute or two later the leathern bags to contain the day's shoot, and our present instalment thereof, were being deposited in the stable of the farmhouse, after which we moved on again. Right opposite us, when orchard and cottage were cleared, was a steep bit of bank, where freshly-moved earth showed that rabbits were in active occupation. There was no chance of approaching this stronghold unseen from our present direction. It was a place for ferreting, rather. We now neared another rivulet. Rough was all excitement, straining to the limit of his leash, yet not violently rebellious of restraint. The principal motioned his friend to advance towards a gap in the thick sycamore hedge. Gun at the ready, he crept forward. We watched alertly. Beyond the hedge seemed to be a small field. The swelling ridge we had been passing here broke into a sheer front, not rocky, but grassy, and decked with hazel and oak and ash, pitted here and there

where the soil perpetually frittered away. This
face of the bluff was likely to be honeycombed
with burrows, and the natural feeding-ground of
their occupants would be the narrow level W——
was reconnoitring. I saw his gun go up, there
was a couple of sharp reports, and W——,
jamming fresh cartridges into the breach, was
plunging across the stony beck course in the hope
of getting a parting shot at some outlier. But if
such there were, it did not come within our range
of vision. W—— mounted the gap and walked
out to 'pick up.' With Rough now at liberty,
questing bramble and bush in a systematic manner
in front of us, we now negotiated the very wobbly
gate (or hurdle) which divided us from the
coppiced bluff. The principal now turned to me.

' Stand well back, and call if Rough drives anything among the bushes.'

The angle of the short rise was so severe that I
could not do this properly till I had retreated into
the bed of the streamlet. Rough was ranging,
often hidden from sight by intervening bushes,
halfway up the slope. From his excited movements, game had apparently been astir not many
seconds ago. Trail after trail he struck, but each
time the makers were safe aground. A moment
of silence, then he gave tongue—a wild, musical
clarion-call to the chase—and with head down and

stern up flashed in and out among the bushes. A
rabbit had crossed the brae in front of him toward
the cluster of burrows opposite which W——
had posted himself. The sudden intrusion of a
bustling enemy roused the rabbits sheltering in
the further half of the coppice, and Rough's
grand voice rang out again and again as he galloped
about.

' Mark, to your left !' The fur was making a
dash across a narrow gap commanded by the distant
gun. W—— slewed around quickly and fired.
His eye was barely off the rolling body ere there
was another sharp rustle among the grass. A
rabbit was descending the brae in a frantic attempt
to reach its hole. The shot, though at very short
range, was not easy, for the rabbit presented a
very foreshortened length, and was moving with
the added impetus of the steep slope.

Rough was still frantically busy among the
undergrowth in the closest part of the coppice.
Rabbits were being dislodged without doubt, but
they were able to get to earth without coming
into our sight. One essayed to break in our
direction, and the beagle, after a sharp backward
glance, allowed it. The principal was ready the
moment cover was left, and did not miss. The
rabbit, though far up the slope when hit, rolled
an inanimate corpse to within my reach.

It was now apparent that the occupants of the bluff-end coppice were thoroughly aroused to their danger, and that scant further toll would be extracted for the present, so we turned back— Rough most regretfully, and only in obedience to many calls and whistles—and surmounted the wobbly fence. At the crest of the bluff we walked across an intervening field to a dense-bottomed hedge, haunt of various outliers from the colony in the wood. One gun took each side the fence, Rough working ahead of them, and myself wandering a bit wide in the hope of flushing a ' clapped 'un ' from the sodden long 'fog' grass. At first Rough didn't seem very willing to work the hedge, probably because no game was there, contenting himself with trotting alongside. But before he had gone thirty yards he was all keenness, wriggling through the smallest smoots (tracks) to change fields every few seconds.

But not a rabbit would budge. For several hundred yards Rough wriggled and scampered, then paused with his nose scenting the air opposite a clump of impenetrable thorns, whimpering, and his lean body quivering with enthusiasm. But I guess this was the haunt of a cute old rascal who, from the secure mouth of his hole, was enjoying Rough's quandary, and every few seconds exposing enough of his unreachable self to taint the air for the beagle's nostrils to snuff. Quite a minute this probable by-play went on, and at the end our white companion moved on again by the hedge-side.

'Stop!' said the principal, close to whom I was walking. Throwing his gun up, he stepped backward some ten yards, his eyes all the while intent on something among the tushes of grass. Then he fired. There was a convulsive moment as a white body rolled over and over. The rabbit was but a small one, and as it lay had quite escaped my notice. Probably forty yards on the same incident occurred, but this time I sighted the frail, white-lined ears like two dead leaves above the grass. It is wasteful to shoot such tiny padders, but as they sit among the grass, with only a pair of ears visible, it is impossible to hazard a guess as to what size the creatures really are. To flush them and give them law in a field full of curious heifers means losing them, or risking serious damage to the bovine spectators.

The hedgerow finished, we turned farmwards, walking fairly wide apart to beat up as much ground as possible. Rough's restless movements on the left sent a big rabbit leaping right across our front. Moving at speed, a rabbit presents much of the poetry of motion. How regularly its limbs curve and straighten, and its lithe body bounds in response to muscles hard as steel hidden beneath the soft gray-and-white fur. Yet this one, though blessed with abundant energy, did not get to cover before the principal's gun spoke.

At the homestead, as it was not yet time for lunch, we deposited our game, and examined the vegetable - garden. It is surprising how often during the noisiest hours of the days rabbits may be flushed from harbours where they must lie in daylong peril from the small host of sheep-dogs ranging all over the place. But to-day Rough pushes through tufts of raspberry-canes and beds of cabbage without a sign of success. Next to the field behind the farm, marching across the tangled tussocks and examining the hedges without raising a flutter. Then down to the barn, where we sat on the hay-seeded floor (for furniture there was none), with the fragrant 'mow' for back-rest, and lunched off an enormous pie.

While this duty was being attended to, the next move was also discussed : the principal, Rough and I were to take another turn at the beckside coppices, while the other gun would try up the glen to the marshy field, our opening place. At the gate out of the fold we separated, but, instead of keeping below the bluff, struck upwards, to where it fell away abruptly. As we stood there, partly hidden by a thick veil of full-leaved sycamore,

we had an almost bird's-view of the little feeding-ground W—— had so completely raked from
the beckside two hours agone. Beyond the hedge,
betwixt wood and field, was a little reddish-brown
patch—almost out of range. If, as to my eye
seemed most probable, this was merely an upturned
sod, to fire would be to startle the outliers to the
burrows. If the patch was really a rabbit, so near
to the cover of the hedge was it that its slightest
leap therewards would cause it to be lost to us.
I was thus undecided ; but the principal, more
accustomed than I to the vagaries of furred
creatures, raised his gun. There was a very slight
movement of the reddish-brown spot — it *was*
a rabbit ; the high-pitched crack of smokeless
powder echoed along the hillside, and the patch
had disappeared. Hit or miss? The fence at
the top of the brae was a stout one ; its top being
wattled into an unbreakable bullfinch to capering
heifers and young horses. I handed the gun over,
then followed suit. Four long, sliding strides
carried us down the worst pitch, and in a few
seconds we were by the watercourse. My companion lay his gun down and climbed over the
hedge to seek his rabbit, a search I prosecuted
among the rank nettles and long tangled grass on
my side, but for some little time neither of us
succeeded. The principal, finishing his side, began

at the opposite end of my more difficult beat. At that moment a rabbit, its eyes glazing in death, rolled out from among the evil-smelling garlic into the beck course not two yards from where I stood. The long shot had therefore gone home.

While we were thus employed, the beagle was enjoying a very lively time on the coppiceside ; twice I saw him scurrying in hot pursuit in a thin scrub of oaks. Our rabbit found, my companion again took up his gun and posted himself on a tiny rise in the path along the beckside, watching where Rough was working. It was, perhaps, three minutes before, with a rush, a rabbit broke cover from a tangle of grass right about our heads ; veiled with bushes as the hillside was, the shot seemed almost an impossible one, but it was essayed. The dull sheen of a clouded sun dwelt upon the slender uplifted double tube of steel ; the muscles of the lean face bending towards the stock of polished wood stiffened ; his keen eye seemed to flash from trigger-lock to sight, and, passing through the thin air, lighted upon the little animal—gray, with white underparts showing as with strenuous haste it trod, perchance for the last time, the well remembered smoot among the tussocks. The glance seemed scarce to have reached the rabbit ere, with a sharp explosion, a tongue of flame spurted from the bright steel chamber. The dead gray stems of

grass crushed and broke as the quivering body
stumbled, checked, then rolled over and over
down the slope. The next rabbit stole softly down
the hedgeside when we had moved to the limit of
the brae. Rough, ranging beyond the fence, was
having our keenest attention as he hunted and
whimpered round a dense clump of alders. I was
standing some yards back, when I heard and
located the stealthy rustle. My call, ' Mark, this
side the fence !' brought the gun round promptly ;
but the rabbit cast all attempts at stealth to the
wind, and scampered straight in our direction.
In a moment it was so near the gun that a shot
would have blown it to pieces. But when it came
within a couple of yards, the furred one whisked
sharply into a smoot through the hedge, and,
without again showing itself, found harbour. Its
escape was deserved for the sharpness of its
manœuvre.

After this Rough's chases began to take him
further afield, and sometimes he ran quite out of
our sight : we could hear his grand voice going
away along the hidden fields. But his journeyings were fruitless. If the scents he was following were fresh, the rabbits merely ran a circle
over the tussocky grass before taking to the
depths of the warrens. Yet his courage never
faltered, and he returned to search new brakes of

bramble and hazel with never-failing patience. Sundry calls and whistles brought him within reach, and, as no other way of getting him away from the coppice offered success, the leash was put on, and away he trotted quietly by my side. But on the outskirts of the woods he was set at liberty again, and marked the period by immediately rousing a somnolent rabbit in the hedgerow across the brook. With glee he chased it up and down, but Bunny did not intend to seek the open. We could hear the crackling of dead twigs as it dashed about the dense tangle ,and Rough's quivering body showed us where approximately it was ; but though up and down the hedge it ran, the sharpest eye could not sight it. Rough never despaired till the rabbit got into some burrow and scent failed. In answer to our call, he then left the hedgeside, and was trotting across the stony bed of the rivulet towards us when several wide-mouthed burrows attracted his attention. In a flash he was struggling into the dark depths, his voice coming back in strange muffled tones as he, scarce a yard within, came to passes so narrow that even his small white body could not advance. In and out, every time with more red soil adhering to his fine coat, right and left, he visited each hole in turn, settling down at last to scratch a way into the wider tunnel. His voice seemed to be constantly ringing

the entreaty, ' Why, why don't you come out ?'
but the rabbits, shivering in their furthest recesses,
did not respond to the urgent cry.

Finding anything short of violence useless to
remove the beagle, we ' left him alone in his glory '
and returned to the farm.

' I wish Rough would be coming,' said my companion a few minutes later, after settling the
routes for himself and the other gun for the rest
of the day, and even as he spoke the beagle
scrambled through the lower bars of the fold gate.
Oh, where was the pretty coat of this morning !
It was damp, and the sandy soil was smeared over
every hair, while muzzle and paws were clotted
with light red mud. But Rough's work had been
so good that nothing could be alleged for a few
such minor indiscretions as this.

The leash was put on, and we left the farmyard.
We struck in a different direction this time, following the course of the little stream. Here and
there alders spring from the water's edge, and
beneath their shade rabbits are fairly sure to be
found. My companion approached with caution,
and, before I had time to get up, fired. I saw the
rabbit roll over, but, acting on instructions, did not
cross the stream to pick it up. Two score yards
lower down, just where the beck ripples from its
shady pools down a long shelving shale, a party of

rabbits were feeding in fancied security. The gun was levelled, and, as the released Rough gave tongue in wilful glee, two short flashes and reports heralded two more successful shots. Not a miss yet to this gun. The long flats were unproductive of sport, but after a while we came to where the bluffs, standing some yards back from the water, were adorned with a sprinkling of gorse.

'We're sure to have some fun here,' said my gun, 'when Rough begins to rustle the whins.'

When my companion had taken up a position on the brink of the rise commanding its whole breast, I let the beagle go. For a few minutes he ravaged fruitlessly about—'not at home' at every seat and smoot. Suddenly Rough, in a ranging rush, balked. There was something alive in a whin in front of it. One moment its eyes scanned the tangle, and located the rabbit more closely; next it turned its head, to assure itself that its master was in position; then, with head lowered, it rushed into the bush. Of course Bunny bolted instantly, laced in and out among the remaining bushes, then broke into the open. A few yards with Rough chasing pell-mell in the rear, then the fugitive seemed to curl up in its mad career, and the dog had gripped it in a moment. It was quite dead by the time I got up. As Rough seemed to be unwilling to work the whins further, we turned aside, crossing the stream and climbing the steep bank beyond.

We crossed the crest and took the lee of the hedge for some way, till a gap where another fence struck at right angles presented a chance for another shot. Turning to the left, we approached the best series of whins on the whole shooting. But here luck deserted us. Rough, hunting among the long storm-broken grass, roused a 'sitter' to flight, and pursued. He was a beagle: calls and whistles did not check him in full chase, and his quarry leapt up quite out of range. Rough's alarming notes had their expected effect. When we came to the edge of the whins, we could hear him 'towrowing' at an unseen distance among the bushes, and there was not a rabbit to be seen. Nor did the partridge, of which for years a covey had inhabited a corner of the next field, appear. We called at several likely places on our return journey to the farm, but every animal was secure in its burrow, and Rough's most agonized searches of hedge-bottoms and becksides was of no avail.

When the morning's bag was reckoned up, we found that nineteen rabbits in all had fallen to our share—not bad for a farm where no kind of preserving is carried on, and for a district where poachers are not scarce.

III. A WINTER DAY'S SPORT

AT sunrise on a summer morning the dewy grass shows where wild game has passed during the hours of darkness; but, though eloquent, these signs speak a language unknowable to the casual observer, and you rarely meet a man so talented as to be able to say with certainty what species have brushed these moist tracks, whose perception is keen enough to note the difference between the traces of rabbit and hare, and who can tell what winged occupant of the preserve alighted here and there. It is only after a thick fall of snow that Nature reveals itself by footprints to anyone who can enjoyably spend an hour or two in the frosty air.

Three inches of snow masked meadow, moor, and mountain, and showed through the acres of leafless coppice. The gamekeeper had prepared for a long tramp, and we proposed to accompany him part of his journey. Though well advanced in middle life, he could still outstride us juniors on the rougher ground, while abrupt ascent or descent, or progress through tangled heather or thicket, taxed him far less than us. As we had the run of the shooting, we took guns with us on even our shortest jaunts; for though game was not abundant (measured by so many head an acre), there was often a curious animal or bird to be got for preservation. In the lane the snow crunched pleasantly beneath our passing feet; but when we began to cross the meadows travelling became heavy, for clods of snow, three inches or so thick, adhered to our boots at every stride. The keeper alone stepped with ease, and we groaned to hear him say that he had taken the precaution to oil the soles of his boots at starting. Our progress was so slow now that we readily agreed to his pushing on, leaving us to follow at our leisure. We touched the first wall a little below its junction with the boundary of the woods. The smooth surface of the field was dotted with long lines of footprints. Rabbits and hares had, in the few hours which had elapsed since the cessation of the storm, been afoot, and here and there little cavities showed where wandering animals had nosed their way through to a few succulent plants available for food. The morning, which had been somewhat dark so far, brightened as the day approached; a stronger light seemed to be spreading along the valley-sides, and the mists which had dimmed the distant lowlands began to rise and recede seawards. At about seven o'clock full day had come, though the sun still tarried; a rosy light was visible even over the head of the great fellside on which we were. The scene was one in which wide snow-fields and dense woodlands, shaggy coppices and huge naked rocks, made splendid contrasts; while the ice-covered pools in the valley beneath took on all the varying, ever-changing tints of the sky above.

My companion had eyes for other things than the exquisite beauty of our surroundings, and as I turned I noticed that he was intently looking at a trail which wound aimlessly in and out among the bushes fringing the main wood. The tracks were deep in the snow—obviously, the animal was of more than the usual weight of the woodland denizens; the prints were joined, as though the foot that made them was not lifted high, but, rather, shuffled from one contact to another. What was it? Last year, the keeper told us, there had been rumour through the countryside that some strange animal occupied the Craigside woods. This was the first sign we had had of the mysterious visitant. The footprints were deep, the marks were connected: a closer look showed that the spoor was that of a small plantigrade—the badger.

Here and there in the open rides we came across labyrinths of footprints : the badger had wandered through one clearing, the tiny paws of the squirrel had pattered along the snow at another place—see where his tail had brushed aside a little ruffle of snow as he passed along. But most of our judgments as to what birds had been present were mere speculation ; and in a short time even my enthusiastic friend took his eyes from the evidences of past presences to look through the groves and up the hillsides for those creatures of which glimpses were now and again to be had. Wild pheasants in their brave plumage called as they ran out of sight or flew up among the trees, a jay screamed as it winged away, and here and there a magpie chattered. Craigside Woods hold game, but much feathered vermin finds home there. It is impossible for the keeper to keep their numbers down without help. Think of an area three miles long and five miles wide—woods, moor, fell, and dale—in the charge of one man, and he hampered by having to rear a thousand pheasants per season. The smaller birds hop sadly from twig to twig, dislodging tiny puffs of snow every time they perch. They, poor things ! suffer during this sort of weather severely, not only from want of food, but from the persecutions of buzzards and sparrow-hawks and others of the falcon kind. At other seasons the lesser birds are able, by reason of corresponding so closely in colour with their environment, to escape serious diminution, but now, when everything is backed by white, there is no such protection. Indirectly to-day the hawks' keenness for harrying brings them little good, as both J—— and myself are able to get good shots and effective. Viewed closely, alive and dead, the sparrow-hawk is a neat bird; its gray-brown and white feathers harmonize quietly and well, and the poise of the body and wings, when alive, are pretty. Then, the speed at which they pounce down on a bird they have selected is worth watching. In the dense larch coppice we hear the cooing of many cushats, but they do not come in sight. In the very darkest dell a rowan-tree has established itself, and on its slender branches still hang a few clusters of what were in autumn bright golden berries, but which by this have lost their lustre. But the tree is alive with the forms of birds, which keep up a low cuttering the while they strip the fruit from the swaying stems.

Beyond the dark wood is a narrow belt of furze and cevins; and at our entering into this domain there is a tremendous rushing of wings as a covey of grouse takes the air just out of effective range. The moor-birds on the most exposed shootings regularly at the approach of the winter famine migrate temporarily to lower and more fruitful grounds. The next incident was the crossing, within a hundred yards of us, of a fox. It leapt out of the wood, and, dodging through the whins, was away for its distant borran [pile of stones] before we had time to move. But as it crossed the hollow in which we were standing we had a good view. At a steady gallop the redskin skimmed along, nor seemed barely to touch the frozen snow; at the edge of the ravine he hesitated a moment, then in two bounds was down the declivity, and nimbly balancing himself on a boulder in the bed of the ghyll. Here he hardly seemed to pause to gather his limbs beneath his body, but without sign of effort jumped well on to the steep bank opposite. As he regained the level of the moor, he resumed the swinging stride which mayhap had during the night carried him a dozen miles away.

The wan sunlight was now streaming over the great scaur on our right; on every foot of the many miles within sight frost spangles glittered; the river pools gleamed like polished silver. On the higher ground the wind had piled many drifts; every rock was plastered white; every bed of heather which had resisted the wind's sweep was swamped in it. Yet from many a long spit of even grass the hindering mantle had been swept, and we walked with more ease than at any part of our journey. To break the death-like stillness of a frozen moor any sound is welcome—the croak of a raven, the bleating of a stray sheep, or the wild skirl of a heron or curlew. It was the first-named sound which attracted our attention. No such bird was visible; the sound seemed to come from over the hillock we were ascending. In a few seconds the bird of ill-omen was viewed by the beckside, busy at some carrion meal. 'Quietly,' whispered my companion. 'I want a raven for my collection.' The dusky one was so intent upon satisfying its appetite that we got well within range before it rose. We had both prepared to fire, though J—— was to have first shot. I kept my eye on the big bird slowly gaining its regular flight, speed, and rhythm; my friend hesitated—perhaps, as he afterwards said, he was in the midst of a shivering bout, and did not care to risk a miss. Probably it was in despair that he discharged one barrel at last in the direction of what was fast becoming a quickly-moving black dot on the white mountainside; but the result was startling. There was a sharp rustle of snow, a crisp crackle of heather branchlets, and a covey of fine grouse shot away, keeping low as they went. They, however, did not get off without paying toll, as both my ready barrels got

home, and J——'s single chamber brought down
a bird. Habit, I suppose, made me exchange the
empty shells for full ones at panic speed (considering the numbness of my ungloved hands),
but the habit was justified by results. The noise
of the routed grouse started the whole stock of
game in the dell: a stray rabbit scurried away
towards the warren five hundred feet lower down
—the choke barrel stopped it, just as I feared
distance was going to bring immunity; a pair
of snipe whirring up from a sphagnum morass got
my other shot. The effect was somewhat curious,
for both birds fluttered away at a slow, painful
pace, evidently hard stricken. The cock-bird
came to earth sixty yards away, but the other,
after a period in which it seemed likely to fall,
gradually regained its customary wing-power, and
we saw it no more. A curlew shot wailing upwards, several plovers added their querulous cries,
and long after we had passed from the glen the
excited bird-calls rang through the clear air.

Meanwhile, scrambling on hands and knees up
the stiffest parts, we had scaled a slack between
two precipices, and by dint of hard work reached
the summit of the mountain. This was not a
very great height, yet commanded an extensive
outlook. To northward lay a rolling moor, its
white expanse broken here and there by gray,

where the heather was only partly buried in the snow, by sharp-cut lines of occasional larch plantations, or by blurs of clustering cevins. Beyond, against the brilliant blue of the sunlit winter sky, stood a great disconnected sea of mountains, their pure white garb varied by irregular blue-black masses—great cliffs on which the snow could find no lodgment. Through the glasses, however, the cliffs were broken up by snow-floored gullies and rock-splits, and traversing ledges carrying fleecy loads, till it seemed as if a white lacework had been drawn across the bold steeps. One peak stood out from the sea of mountains, lording it over a series of minor but rugged hills. On both sides, deep below, were snow-bound valleys, and in the distance, dark and leaden, beyond the brightening power of the winter sun, the sea. On isolated shoulders of the moors one or two bright dots showed mountain tarns not yet frozen completely over, and like ribbons of silver the main streams wound down the valleys. On this upland the air was still, and hardly a sound came to our ears. At any other season the rivulets dashing and fretting down their rocky courses would have been easily heard, but now they were frozen. At any other season the numerous sheep grazing about the hills and slopes would have sent up occasional bleats; but these were now far away—

driven to the valleys on the approach of winter. Gone, too, were the hawks and ravens and foxes, and the other wild creatures of the uplands, nearer to the haunts of men, where the means of subsistence were procurable.

Our glasses ranged over the wide area in view : little dots in far-off meadows enlarged into men and animals, the shepherd dragging the small hay-ration from the stackyard to his flock, the other servants doing the various offices of the farms. One house seemed to be the rendezvous for men and dogs slowly dragging across snow-covered fields. When a small crowd had collected, we watched it leave the farmyard and strike into the belt of larches, above which, somewhat scattered, it appeared, moving faster and apparently without any canine following. Instantly it came to me what was occurring—we were witnessing one of the ruthless informal fox-chases for which the district is famous. A fox had been plundering hen-roosts in its bloodthirsty fashion. A pack of canines — collies, hounds, bobtails, cross-breds, terriers, of all denominations and sizes, anything that could scent and run—had been collected, put on the red-hot trail, and were now streaming somewhere in front of those careering dots, pursuing the redskin, who, after a night's blood orgie, was at a terrible disadvantage. But, though again and again we swept the bare hillside with our glasses, the scratch pack eluded our vision, and it was not till they had gone some two miles that we detected them. A number of restlessly moving dots was dashing about a big borran or moraine of stones in which, seemingly, the fox had taken refuge. They were almost opposite us, across the gulf of the dale, and in full sight. We watched the men come up at their best speed and examine the heap of stones. Apparently the chief entrance was on the side nearer us, as they clustered mainly in that direction. Man after man knelt down among the snow, and through the still air came faint echoes of their shouts encouraging the terriers presumably at work deep below. But now the men come away from Reynard's fastness, and we watch anxiously to see him, worried by his enemies, make a bolt for life. But this he does not do, and a few minutes later a figure detaches itself from the group and moves swiftly along the ridge, disappearing from ken near the top of a sharp peak. His comrades stand idly about the borran, save one or two who return to the opening among the rocks to egg on the unseen terriers. It is quite a long time before the man we watched away returns with what appears to be a stick in his hand—a crowbar, by means of which the stones of the fox's fortress will be prised asunder. Instantly the whole company is at work, two working the lever, the others throwing out the stones dislodged. Ten minutes' frenzied labour sees a huge gap in the heap of stones; there is a sudden movement among the men; their dogs, which have been lying in odd hollows in the snow, cast themselves into the group; the air is rent with a wild yell. Then all is peace to us, but an oscillating, tearing patch of dog-flesh marks where Reynard's carcase is being fought for. 'Chopped at a borran' is the fate of many a redskin wanderer of great and evil repute among the mountains.

We have stood so long watching the events of this fierce hunt that our limbs (unbeknown to our excited selves) have long been gripped by the frosty air; our attempts at walking bring excruciating pains, which gradually lose sting, however, as the stagnant blood is forced through the veins of leg and arm and shoulder.

We had completely banished our chill, and were walking along the hillside, gradually trending downwards, when I was surprised to note a little mountain tarn almost at our feet. So close enfolded was it in the swelling ridges that we had not suspected its existence. But pleasure was added to the scene by the fact that on a small patch of unfrozen water were several dark moving bodies—water-fowl of some sort inviting a stalk. We turned abruptly down the slope, going far to the right in order not to disturb our game. When beneath the level of the tarn, we turned into a dell, where rattled a meagre rivulet—the escaping surplus from the lakelet above. In the shelter of this watercourse we hoped to get within shooting distance, but after a hundred yards we had had enough of the scramble. The gully was floored with huge boulders, which, now sheeted with snow and ice, presented slippery faces in every direction, and every foot and handhold had to be carefully scraped. The problem which finally baffled us was to compass a pool occupying the whole width of the ravine, while from its brink the cliffs rose sheer, presenting not a vestige of hold. I tried a dozen methods to circumvent the cornice, but failed. It was quite anxious work descending the ice-sheathed rocks, but after some twenty minutes we were on the whitened hillside again, greatly chagrined that the ducks were to escape. I persisted that another approach to the tarnside more feasible than the river-bed might be found. It was in half-despair that we skirted the ridge bounding the tarn-basin, but in a minute or two my companion, whose high spirits had been somewhat dashed by our failure, jerked my arm. Carefully reconnoitring from the shelter of a summit, he had noticed a shallow furrow in the snow which promised an approach. It did not take more than five minutes for us to reach its depths, when we found that the hollow reached quite down to the water's edge, and that our advance would in large measure be covered by boulders and dense bushes. We were within fifty yards of the water when all shelter was passed; in front lay an unwrinkled drift. I opined that, by crawling along to where a low wall had been erected for more luxurious and leisurely shooters, we would be able to get to the waterside. It was chilly work and tedious : care, above all, had to be taken of our guns, for a speck of snow in the barrel might mean a dangerous burst. Anyhow, half frozen to the elbow, we had almost worked to our desired haven before the sounds of duck came to our ears. The birds were feeding in the next bay to that we were so toilsomely approaching, and our present goal would be of little use to shoot from. Therefore we patiently skirted the snow-filled wall and got to the side of a little ridge dividing their bay from ours. J—— was in advance, and moved so incautiously that he had exposed his presence to the birds before I got near. I heard a sharp clan-call, a splashing and a rustling of wings, and the flock, I knew, were away. J—— fired twice, and, leaping forward—caution was useless now—I espied the birds in time to add a shot. However, only one bird fell, and it lay on the thin ice edging the water. To retrieve it was a task requiring great nicety of movement, and after many failures the ice immediately round the body was separated from the sounder surface, and floated to within reach of a rock not far from the side. This trophy secured, we were again afoot.

The day which broke so fair and bright was now becoming cloudy; the mists gradually crept into the distant mountains, and descended to one peak after another, till it became apparent that the ground on which we were standing would ere long be enveloped in shifting gray. This was the more disquieting because we had rambled far from the direction we had intended, and a lofty ridge stood between us and our home. It was imperative that we should pass this before the clouds fell so far, so up we climbed, making for where we thought the path to our valley lay. Long ere we reached the crest of the slope the dusky masses had fallen around us, and we walked in semi-darkness. At first we could still see some fifty yards through the creeping mist; then it closed down further, and everything beyond a radius of a score yards was blotted out. When, however, the breeze began to be filled with fine

snowflakes, this tiny circle was narrowed till my
comrade, two gun-lengths away, was little more
than a darker shadow. We tramped upwards for
forty minutes; then the slope changed direction
—we had passed the ridge, evidently—and we
turned to the left. Some half-hour later we
judged that we should be in the proximity of
our path and clear of the cliff, so we attempted
very, very cautiously a descent. The slope was
steep, and careful stepping was required to guard
against slipping. We had perhaps ventured thirty
yards, when the angle of descent became dangerous,
and I called a halt. J—— asserted that our valley
was right below, and we would soon get to less
abrupt ground. I had my doubts as to the latter
point, and emphatically refused to risk reaching
home by way of a three-hundred-foot drop down
the rocks. We argued the point; then J—— gave
way. Further and further to our left we patrolled
without much success, then rested a moment in
the whirling snow. We were inordinately puzzled
as to our whereabouts, for we had expected to find
here a wide, easily-falling sweep of hillside instead
of a rocky precipice.

'Why, we must have been wandering in a
circle!'

Yes, there, not ten yards below, the thickening
mantle of snow had not yet completely blurred

our footprints of half an hour agone. We were surprised indeed. Now carefully checking our progress at every few paces, we soon came to easier ground, and at last reached the mountain-path we were in search of. It was level with snow, and somewhat bad to follow, yet it served to shortly bring us below the clouds. A thin snow-shower was passing up the valley, dimming the distance, but this was soon over and the sun shone out anew. But the clouds clung to the upper slopes of our mountain for the rest of the day.

Our bag weighed somewhat heavily ere we covered the three miles to our quarters, but we regretted this little. When we came below the clouds, the first living thing in sight was a raven, next a curlew, and then a flock of wild-swans swooping down to some unfrozen marsh. After this we cleared the snow carefully from our gun-barrels, and nothing more important than a black-bird was seen.

IV. On the Frozen Meres

DAY after day the cold increased. The lake-shore was fringed with ice; in the thin sere woods the trodden leaves crackled crisp underfoot. Then one morning the landscape was blotted out with a slow whirl of white, hastened by scarce a breath of wind. It was delightful to climb up to the moor as the white fleece piled up by inches. The larch-wood at a hundred yards was a dim meaningless shadow, yet we discovered unexpected beauties. During the night the snowfall ceased; the moon set as the day broke. A freezing breeze crept over the miles of snow, and, as it met tarn or beck, congealed their surfaces. On the broad lake the ice-sheet thus encouraged spread even at the height of noon, while after the sun set, and while the bright silent stars looked down, the frost realm extended apace.

Next morning the air was clear. Miles upon miles of white mountain-slopes extended along the horizon; woods and fields alike were buried

in snow. Everything seemed pure against the
steel blue of the ice-bound lake, or the lighter
blue out there where the ducks disported in water
as yet unapproached by Winter's fetters. The ice,
though in places sound, was still unsafe where
the tiny mountain streams poured in. Yet, with
caution, we skated on mile after mile, the sound
of steel now ringing through the snow-floored
woodland rides, now echoing away across the wide
area of ice as we ventured further from shore.
An island was now in front, crowned with dark
spruces save on the north-west corner, where
many centuries ago some Norseman cleared a
space for his habitation. The erection had gone
long before the earliest histories were written, but
the location was proved by the stray scraps of
iron which the builder had used to bind the
rough timbers together. As we swing along the
smooth ice, always keeping outside the narrow
snow-covered ribbon, we think of the Norseman's
iron nails, then of the bloomeries (small smelting
furnaces) established by these shores centuries
later under the supervision of the Abbot of
Furness—in days when it was profitable to bring
the iron ore to the woods to be purified with
charcoal. The industry seems not yet to be
extinct, for as we glide round a rocky naze into a
large bay, the faint breeze carries into our faces

a pungent burden of wood-smoke. And there ahead are half a dozen eddying columns rising from as many pyres.

Charcoal - burning is still an active industry in several of our old-world countrysides. The coppices are allowed to grow for fifteen years, at the end of which, the chief stems being some four inches thick, they are felled. The wood-cutters divide the trunks into short sections, which are peeled of their bark, and laid while still moderately green in cone-shaped piles, hollow to provide for a draught. When the cone is completed it is thatched with turf, all air being excluded except from the centre, where the fire is kindled. When this has thoroughly got ' hod,' as the woodsmen say, the ventilating - shaft is closed.

The fire within now smoulders away, throwing off dense volumes of smoke through the inter-stices of the sods. Thus the oven will go on for several days, during which period considerable vigilance is required. At times, fanned by the wind, the buried fire gains power, and, if not duly checked, is apt to burn through the coating of sods and send out a ruddy tongue of flame. This activity causes a chemical change, rendering the contents of the oven valueless as charcoal. To prevent these outbreaks, the charcoal-burner keeps on hand a number of damp sods, which he places as required upon overheated points. The other extreme, preventing sufficient ventilation, is quickly marked by a decreasing spiral of smoke, noting which the burner simply removes a turf or two from the covering of the pile till the fire has regained power and heat.

A call brings the charcoal-burner outside the rough hut of poles and brushwood from which he is watching his fires. In a few minutes our skates are off and we are climbing the steep to him. He says that since our last visit two of his ovens have died out; combustion has ceased, and a quantity of charcoal is fairly won. From this open-fronted hut—he has several, to protect him from changes of the wind — he can see every fire. 'I'm frightened that one there is going to get into a low [flicker of flame],' he says as, sod in hand, he goes to the cone in question. The man speaks in a grand native dialect, without pride or apology in his words—a burly man in middle life, tanned and weather-beaten, roughly but warmly dressed and shod. In his face is the good humour of a heart where reigns perennial spring; his voice is full and resonant; his eye beams with health and the contentment of outdoor life.

He is loath to speak of the romance of his own life. 'Nay, nay,' he will reiterate, 'there's naught

new in the woods. Year after year goes, and
not an alteration, save that coppices spring and
are felled, and men grow older.' But he can be
more easily drawn to speak of Lanty Slee, the
last known illicit distiller among the mountains,
and how he oft escaped capture ; of the many
'mains' of cock - fighting still to be seen from
the retirement of a charcoal-burner's hut. The
Hermit of the Woods forty years ago was a
friend of John's, and he still treasures an oak
staff which that curious character presented him.
A broad spiral of black, perhaps 'done with
smoke,' as Friend John thinks, decorates it,
proving that the Hermit was not without knowledge of some secret crafts.

The charcoal-burner is a keen naturalist in his
way. It was John who for a number of years
held to the statement that the badger frequented
our lonelier woods. His observation is now con-
clusively proved, and to-day he shows us a dell
where a plantigrade has been recently afoot. ' I
heard a wild swan whooping this morning,' he
adds with marked satisfaction. ' There's a stiffish
frost astir when they come so low.' But the
charcoal-burner's craft he will say little of, and
what wonder, if he cannot raise enthusiasm on
it ? For hours during the recent snowfall he was
patrolling round his fires, checking this and

encouraging that to greater heat. Even now, in his airy tepee of brush, he is at the same moment chilled with the frosty air and warmed with the fierce heat of the fire whereon a battered black kettle is beginning to boil preparatory to the noonday meal.

During summer, he states, the life is grand. For weeks on end John camps in the woods, a free gipsy. A flitch of bacon, a bag of flour, are provision for a month. If the woodsman needs variety, there are plenty of trout to be caught with a night-line in the nearby streams. It is in late autumn and early winter that the charcoal-burner is most busy. His wreaths of smoke climb upward from the bare spaces once occupied by flourishing woodlands. The march of the seasons in the woods and by the lake is closely noted by John, whose naturalist ear notes which birds trill and which are silent, whose eye sees the coming and going of the migrants. The pipits and the thrushes leave the moors and the bushes, the wagtails the watersides, and in their places, from the far north-east, come the snow-bunting and the fieldfare and various species of duck.

John is now ready to patrol his circle of fires. By the side of the first, however, we pause a moment, for it is laid on the flat crest of a sharp rock-spur. To right and left the slopes are bleak and dismal; the mask of snow cannot hide the scar of the woodcutter, the stumps of sapling oak and hazel and ash. At our feet the lake extends, a long narrow sheet, its head far away in the lap of the snowy mountains. Three more of the charcoal-ovens are on this level. John strides on ahead through the clinging snow, and is attending to the second fire by the time we reach it. Between this and the third we cross a small brook just below a waterfall. John says that the scene from this point was a favourite with the Hermit of the Woods, who on more than one occasion painted it. But we are perhaps more interested in the doings of a tiny dipper which, alarmed at our presence, flirts hither and thither about the pool beneath the fosse. One moment it dives, to reappear right among the frothing, tumbling waters. Next it dances about a snow-covered stone almost level with the pool. Finally, with an impatient trill, it wings its way upstream to where strangers do not pry.

John, like other wood and dale dwellers, cannot understand the greatness of that philosopher (John Ruskin) who for so many years was his neighbour. The musings and wanderings of that master mind were beyond him; yet, if the mind was incomprehensible, I think the man was frequently understood. John tells one story which cannot be too often repeated. One hard winter a labourer, having to provide for a large family, went to the Master of Brantwood to seek some little job till the frost broke. The Professor received the man kindly, and, after giving him a meal, took him to a little flat just above the level of the lake. 'Dig here,' he said. The man got tools and commenced work, and for several days he kept on digging. When the hole got too deep for him to throw the soil and stones out, he got a ladder and a bucket, and so kept on, bringing up the loose stuff in driblets. At last, when he had got down some thirty feet, he reached bed-rock. He then went up to Brantwood, and reported the circumstance to the Professor, who returned with him to the lake-shore. The great man looked into the dark hole a moment, then turned to the labourer, and said : 'Very good ; fill it up again.' John, the charcoal-burner, can think of no reason for the Professor's strange fancy, but he applauds the action, for it kept the poor labourer at work during a long spell of frost, and prevented the poignant misery which ' out of work ' entails on such a man's family.

As John concluded his simple story we came to the last of the ovens, and here we parted, the charcoal-burner to return to his vigil-hut on the rocky spur, we to resume our skates for the five miles' homeward journey.

A year later I was in the neighbourhood of a large and somewhat inaccessible mountain tarn. A spell of dry frost had set in, and as yet no snow had fallen. On the first evening of my sojourn I left my lodgings about six o'clock ; it was quite dark in the hollow, and where the trees thronged I had difficulty in keeping on the open road. In ten minutes I had emerged from the lower ground, and was striding along a moorland road, crossing a tongue of high ground which divided upper and lower valleys. The stars shone bright above, the regiment of massive fells bounding the dale was capped with frost-rime almost as pure as snow ; here and there, contrast to the swelling, soaring contours, were tumbled rocky bields ; a hundred yards beneath my path, at the foot of a steep slope covered with tangled frozen bracken, rattled the stream in its bouldery course. The great gulf of the dale ahead was filled with a gray gloom, which the tiny lamps of heaven could not dispel. My path gradually descended to the level of the stream, fording here and there courses from which the torrents had ebbed. A crash and a tinkle of shivering ice told me when I met these skeletons of former greatness. I had got three miles up the dale, and had banished by exercise the cold from my limbs, before I came to my objective. A single stone arch spanned a rock-chasm at the bottom of which a deep pool churned and gurgled. So deep was the dusk reigning here that only when an upspringing jet caught the vagrant starlight could I accurately determine the depth. Here and there, in the recesses of the rocks, the spray had formed huge icicles ; one was shaped, as it seemed to me, like the fantastic wraith of an enormous man. From this bridge I had intended to return, but ultimately decided, as there was plenty of time, to go forward some little way. I walked sharply— the freezing air permitted no loitering—and, between a couple of big boulders, rounded the corner, and in a few minutes was out in a level hollow.

The scene in front was quite the wildest I have met with : save the stream gurgling over a bed of shingles, there was scarce a sound to be heard. The folded flocks were silent, the ' low, continuous murmurings ' of the fellside torrents were hushed, the very air was held in a frosty stillness. But the sky—here at last was a clear view to where the primrose of the aurora gleamed and faded and gleamed anew. The whitened mountain-peaks seemed rimmed with a wandering, golden irradiance for a moment ; then the hues died away, leaving a chilling aspect before my eyes. Eastward, lo! along the hill-tops ran a line of fire, and the sky above was glowing. Moonrise! Now backward to quarters as smartly as foot can spurn the iron road.

Next morning, skates in hand, we took the direction of the mountain tarn. For nearly two miles our way held up a side-valley, in which were two or three sheep-farms. Here the shepherds were at work carrying huge bundles of hay to their flocks. Now we reached the open moor. The frost-rime lay thick on every blade of grass, and as we climbed higher the air seemed to turn colder. The path was so littered with loose stones that we shortly abandoned it, and struck up the steep slope more directly. In half an hour we stood upon a shelf in the mountainside which commanded a full view of the glen, and of miles of gray-white mountains around it. The worst of the ascent over, we struck across the frozen bogs, and very shortly stood by the mountain tarn. Seen from the beach near its outflow, it was a splendid sheet of ice, without a crack or a flaw anywhere. Its bluish surface seemed to extend a great distance into the lap of some great rocky bluffs. In a few seconds our skates were fixed on; our hands, unspoiled by the false luxury of gloves, were not numbed and nerveless. Despite the cold air circulating about us, we were distinctly warm with the exertions of our brisk climb. How the echoes resounded the ringing sound of steel meeting ice! A buzzard hawk, perched on the tip of a crag five hundred feet above us, took fright and threw itself into the air. For awhile it seemed as though other bird-life was absent. We coasted along cautiously a hundred yards to prove the soundness of the ice; then, as our confidence rose, extended our journeyings, though still keeping on the lower section of the tarn. The only island on this water is a small outcropping patch of rock, without a bush, but the inland home and breeding-place of a family of gulls. We skated out to this and passed around it. So far we had not seen the trace of a skate-track; we were the pioneers here, and, if I knew the dalesmen aright, no other skaters were likely to enjoy this delight.

Fully satisfied as to our security, we now set out to skate right round the sheet of ice, my friend leading. Now and again we passed over areas of Jack Frost's most delicate tracery in hoar: thin white lines joining the most elaborate little 'knobs' of frost-rime, which, examined closely, bore close relation to the beautiful structure of a flower. There was a subdued croaking going on in front; the still air carried sound so well that we skated with the utmost care forward. Both of us hoped to see a raven and were not disappointed.

SPORT AMONG THE FELLS

As we swept into a shallow rock-fringed bay the bird rose with rapid wing from his feast of frozen mutton. A dead sheep lay within ten yards of the shore, gnawed and torn by a dozen tribes of mountain-dwellers. Occasionally from a spot like this a winter wanderer may scare a fox, but generally Reynard eats his fill during the hours of darkness and in some snug corner of the rocky hillside above is sleeping. Our run up the shore of the mere was fairly rapid, but I did not expect our view to have changed so completely. We were now in the upper part of the tarn ; two jutting crags approached and narrowed its centre. The hillsides were strewn with great blocks of stone, tributes from the huge cliffs overhanging them. A deep narrow glen ran up some way from the head of the tarn, then suddenly ceased as a mountain-front arose. Feeding in the burn were birds—a gaunt heron the chief. The little knot of wild-duck did not take alarm till we had run close enough to admire their gorgeous sheeny plumage and soft contours. At the opening of one bay I halted a few seconds and looked through the clear ice beneath me. An unseen current was moving a tangle of yellow water-weeds and, almost touching them was a large pike. A sharp tap on the ice with my skate sent him sheering out into the deep waters. In shallow dubs I have frequently seen the same thing, but not on large tarns. For some time we had been striking in the direction of a high front of rock which rose sheer from the water. Its front, seared with a vein of brilliant white felspar, had been a landmark to us. Isn't it curious to stand on a sheet of thin ice and look down into the inky depths? There we could see, for twenty feet, ledge after ledge and slab below slab, but not the foundation of the rock itself. The ice all round had been in splendid condition, and now we simply flew along beneath the frowning scaurs towards the beach we started from.

Arriving here, skates were doffed and we made down the rugged path again to the dale. Our experience had been an enviable one : there had not been a single drawback. The travelling was rugged enough to keep us warm, the skating glorious. When shall we have such another time ?

AMONG UNDERGROUND SCENERY

AMONG UNDERGROUND SCENERY

THE whole district of Craven, in North-western Yorkshire, is honeycombed with innumerable earth-chambers. Ribblesdale, Wenningdale, Wharfedale, and half a score of other dales named after their respective rivulets, are undermined and tunnelled for miles by the hand of Nature, and beneath their surfaces flow 'sunless streams,' no one knows whither, and measureless to man. Often, in wandering over the mountains there, we hear voices and gurglings from torrents which never find their way at all to the upper world, and from out one cavernous mouth in the hill Whernside flows a stream which in flood-time washes out periodically old silver coins of the reign of Edward I., from some long-lost treasury.

Near Giggleswick Scar is an ebbing and flowing well of exceedingly irregular habits. If you lay your ear to the ground at a certain spot in Ribblesdale, you will hear how the water comes down at Lodore in fairyland, although not so much as a rivulet is to be seen outside of Robin Hood's Mill.

Sometimes tremendous funnels, 200 feet in depth, lead by a very direct route, and one which would take no time at all to traverse, right down upon these mysterious streams. Black and deep enough the water seems, as we peer over the edges of the 'pot' at it, nor does it make one at all ambitious for subterranean exploration. Hellen Pot, which contains in it an underground waterfall of no less than 40 feet, has been descended to the depth of 330 feet, where the black river revolves in a quiet pool, and does not reappear to mortal eye for more than a mile. Some few of these 'pots' have fish in them ; large black trout abound in Hurtle Pot, where the boggart, in rainy weather, is heard to threaten and fret, and are also found in less quantity in the chasm above it, though the upward force of the water is there so strong as to cast up stones of considerable size to the surface, and even on to the bank.

These are some of the wonders within reach of Ingleton : Yordas Cave is perhaps the most wonderful of all. If you are awheel, you turn westward from the village to Thornton-in-Lonsdale. At the church here — note the ancient stocks still standing at the crossways for the punishment of malefactors — your road turns northward up a formidable hill. As seen from the summit of this, Kingsdale presents a wild, and to some folks a dreary, appearance. On the occasion of my visit mist-clouds hung low, and even the lower hills about the valley could scarce be seen. The lower part of the descent is easily rideable, and ere long you are pedalling along a fair moorland road. Around you belts of lime-stone at regular intervals seam the hillside, while closer are the dry brown stones of a river-bed. This is but one of Ingletonia's many freaks ; a mile back were anglers plying their craft. After a wet period this river-bed flows with a torrent, but in a few hours the overplus has dwindled away. The becks on all the surrounding hillsides disappear down rock-chines as they near the dale, to rise to the surface again, perhaps, a couple of miles away.

Opposite the first house in the valley is a notice-board, 'Apply here to view Yordas Cave.' I crossed the fields to Braida Garth House in accord-ance. Here I found Mr. Batty willing to guide me, and to give me any information in his power. Various photos and plans of the cave were shown me, and it was only after an hour's interesting chat that we got under way. My cycle was now left behind, and we made 'crow-drive' for a larch-plantation a mile away. As we passed along the fields, mine host pointed out the locality of various 'pots' on the opposite fell. Rowton

Pot, he assured me, was the deepest yet discovered among the Craven hills. From the ground to where its tributary rills sink out of sight and sound it descends 365 feet! It starts on the top of a ridge, and its bottom is 20 feet below the level of the stream in the valley beneath. About 100 feet down, Mr. Batty informed me, there was a natural bridge across the chasm.

After crossing the fields we reached the dale-road, leaving this at last opposite the larch planting. A wide gully, bristling with rocks and fairly steep, leads you toward shadowy sylvan recesses, and just as these are closing round, Mr. Batty turns to the left with a 'Here we are.'

In the cliff you note a receding gap where the stone has crumbled away. This is the entrance to the cave. As you approach closer, you discover that a way has been dug here. There are steps, and at the foot a cave. Standing there, awaiting the naphtha-lamp Mr. Batty is kindling, you hear the mysterious droning voice of the great giant Yordas calling you to beware. But when, with a tallow candle in your hand, you pass the opened gate, the great Norwegian has withdrawn, though signs of his recent presence are with you for a long time. The throat of the cavern is some twelve feet wide, and perhaps six to ten feet high. There is no crawling to be done between dripping rocks and slimy floors. But a word to anyone who goes cave-exploring : the mud you are footing is very slippery, and care must be constantly taken to prevent downfall.

Mr. Batty ceases swinging the guttering light as he stands opposite a curiously-shaped rock. 'This is the Flitch of Bacon,' he said. Probably the giant was too much disturbed at our ingress to remove it, I thought ; but on touching it, alas! it was of stone. The wily Norwegian did not trust Yorkshiremen or chance intruders. In rapid succession the Brown Bear and the Organ-Pipes were discovered, some distance apart, and with— greatest find of all—the Giant's Hand between. Now I paused at all this, and pondered how such things could be ! Yes, surely the giant, at the first distant sound of our approach, had been grinding out a tune that his pet bear might dance before him. Then, when the clashing of the sundered bars aroused him to his danger, with his left hand the full power of his patent refrigerator, and so instant was that power in action that Bear and Organ and Hand that had just left the gleesome turning of the handle were solidified ere another movement could be made. Then, as befits the grim ogre of a fairy domain, he abandoned the useless limb and fled.

But while I am piecing the story together

my companion is detailing another labyrinth of evidence : The White Bear perilously anchored to an iceberg ; a Lion—or is it a wolf?—ranging in stalactitic majesty along the cave wall. While Yordas was directing his circus, this stony-hearted beast was arguing which way the river flowed with a white lamb (the story is ancient, ergo the lamb has become an aged Horned Ram). But at the alarum of our approach the debate was adjourned *sine die*, probably because the Ram took refuge beneath the Canopy, while his tormentor chased in the direction of the Chapter-House (which, had he had his way, would speedily have become a charnel-house). The next relic, Mr. Batty informed me in an awed voice, is the Pulpit, or Throne ; it is yet dinted with the impression of Yordas's feet, for here he stood till the storming of the cave began.

From gay to grave, from the realms of fairy-land to the hard facts of cave scenery, is always a difficult transition in such a locality as this. We are now standing in the Chapter-House. The light of the naphtha-lamp rises high, but not high enough to discover the roof. At a neck-tiring angle you watch fluted walls rising into far-away darkness. How wonderful is this modelling, done by Nature's own forces! Water, holding lime in solution, trickles plentifully down the rocks. A crevice, a protrusion, however small, arrests its course, and a load of white molecules is deposited as drop by drop percolates down, till a crust of creamy white rounds off the awkward angle. The smallest obstacles cause the magic flutings. A thousand minute springs are, as we stand, busily extending the columns of the Chapter-House. Large ledges are coated with limy deposit ; the outward extensions, as their foundations fail, droop over and fall into such formation as a fair representation of a bunch of bananas (christened two centuries syne the Hive of Bees). Through the gap between the Pulpit and the other wall we look into outer darkness, where the rays of our lamp are seemingly swallowed up. Then Mr. Batty kindles a piece of magnesium wire. In a moment the gurgling, yellow naphtha glow is transcended by a bright flare, which discovers, as you watch, pillars and encrustations suspended on the ones you have admired. The blaze rises higher, and the roof of the Chapter-House, some sixty feet above the damp floor, is seen. What a mysterious vault this must have appeared to a traveller of a hundred years ago, whose power of lighting was limited to a dozen tallow candles like the one in your hand ! Every yard of the cliff is coated with creamy lime, on which, like diamonds, the sliding droplets reflect the intense light. Again and again the coil of wire is resorted to, and the eye wanders toward the gap to the greater cave. The top stone of the Pulpit throws a gaunt shadow across a bed of sand and shingle, in the midst of which a rivulet babbles briskly along. The strong shaft of light also reveals a dim, mysterious distance, where a congregation of rocks rises up to a world of gloom.

Mr. Batty's pyrotechnics being completed, he leads towards the dark rivulet, which to me rather gives a sombre thought. Coming in full vigour from a crevice in the rocks, with a hurrying, worrying gait it crosses that leviathan room, and a screen of rock acts as a barrier to those who would see whither it is hastening. How like to the fretful rush of every-day existence! By a plank we cross the stream and make toward a hole in the limestone wall.

All the time we have been in the cavern the sound of rushing, falling waters has been in our ears. At first it rumbled in a quiet monotony, fraught with a crashing note of warning; now the sound seems changed to the loud threatenings of some ancient Druid—of Yordas, maybe, hero-god of the dale. Three steps lead into a recess. Down my neck a copious splash of water pours. The 'inner circle' of the cave's delights is guarded after rain by a veil of falling drops. Then walk along a wood bridge, and look up. Mr. Batty's naphtha-lamp illumines a narrow rift in the bowels of the mountain. In front from an unseen height a stream is rushing down fifty feet of rock. The air is filled with spray as the curtain of water is torn and buffeted by rock ledges, and thrown out of its course. The whole 'Chapel of the Force' is not ten feet square at its base, and the great converging slabs of rock continue up and up till they seem to meet in darkness. Why cannot we be content with the lights of our forefathers? Had the ceilings of the Chapter-House not been revealed by the brilliance of modern fireworks, how imposing the recollection would have been! And here, where the water spouts from a dim height, churning down among fragments half unseen, the same thing occurs. It shows a great interval riven between two huge columns of rock, and that the leaping torrent issues from upper blackness through it—shows that even this cleft has a visible roof fifty or sixty feet away. But if magnesium's steady combustion destroys delusions of immeasurable height and breadth, it also accentuates the beautiful gouge-marks on the damp walls, the proofs of an age's activity by the cascade. I cannot describe the scene : for a moment the roar of the torrent seeming to slacken, then bursting into a climax of rattle and splash and tinkle almost before the ear had noted the slackening sound; the stream dashing headlong, and jetting from fragments and ledges into a continuous pearly mist; the grim, immovable seams of tough limestone, with here and there a splintered fissure or cornice torn away.

After a long pause we turned away, passed down a narrow pathway, and reached the floor of the cathedral cave again. Our lamp seemed to dwindle in importance, feebly illumining the grotesque stones on the far side of the vault.

'How grand this would seem if the whole cave could be lit up at once!' I remarked to Mr. Batty.

'I've seen it properly lit,' was his reply; 'but it's many a year ago. A few younger dalesmen hauled an empty tar-barrel from the farm into the cave. On a bonfire in the middle we placed it, and while the timber and tar lasted the light was splendid.' Ah me! I remember the flickerings and booming explosions of light attending such a burning. How the great leaping flames would gild that giant dome, and send fugitive shadows dancing in mad riot among the pinnacles and pendant stalactites around! Mr. Batty showed me the Dropping-Well and another allegorical limestone—to me it seemed like the contour of a virgin, backgrounded by a gouge-work reredos. Then we came to the rivulet again ; and here, nearly on a level with the sand-floor, my guide pointed out a confusion of paint-marks. Little colour there was left, but the paint had preserved the stone from the usual washing. '. . . Painter, Burton-in-Lonsdale, 1812,' is, after much adjusting of light, finally shadowed on the slab. In ninety-one years Yordas Cave has presumably become one-sixteenth of an inch wider, for the paint-preserved portions are embossed to half that extent. The rivulet sinks out of view behind a lowered portcullis of rock ; there is a large flow to-day, else, Mr. Batty assured me, we could have crawled down a mile of tunnel to open air. Baffled here, we retrace our steps to the bridge, cross the stream, and slowly make for the throat of the cave. Mr. Batty hangs up the pole he carries to elevate his lamp to the level of the chief encrustations, and as he does so he turns the light on to a medley of uncouth paint-marks.

'Wait a minute! I can read them,' I remark, for the slant of light brings them up clearly. 'Initials, and date 1730.'

To Mr. Batty this is news, for no other date than that by the waterfall has been noted. My tallow-dip is pretty soon glancing a feeble ray against the smooth rock. About eighteen inches above the present floor is a jumble of hieroglyphs of various ages—1730, 1675, and, earliest of all, 1653. The last date had been the handiwork of one Robert Whitandal. (Quoth Mr. Batty: ' The Whitandals once were well known in this valley ; a family lives nearby even now. They are said to have held much property here once, and within my recollection one of the name was steward for this estate.') Robert Whitandal had put some labour into his handiwork, an attempt at a double triangle and an ornamental initial I being added. Another dales family was represented by the name of Robert Foxcroft; the rest were either indecipherable or initials only. Most of the cuttings are now level, or even above the level of the stone; the chisel or knife has pressed the yielding stone to a somewhat tougher consistency than the surface around.

After this my guide departed, and I returned alone to Braida Garth, remounted my wheel, and returned to Ingleton.

Naturally, I was proud of my discovery of the new dates. The last flood in the cave had probably washed the accumulated grit away and allowed me the honour. But on looking into an old book of descriptions, published by Thomas West in 1795, I saw the following :

' *The Western Side of the Cave.*—This is a solid